Integrating the Visual Arts
Across the Curriculum

Integrating the Visual Arts Across the Curriculum

An Elementary and Middle School Guide

JULIA MARSHALL

With contributions by
Ann Ledo-Lane and Elizabeth McAvoy

Foreword by
Connie Stewart

TEACHERS COLLEGE PRESS

TEACHERS COLLEGE | COLUMBIA UNIVERSITY
NEW YORK AND LONDON

Published by Teachers College Press, 1234 Amsterdam Avenue, New York, NY 10027

Front cover design by Julia Marshall. Background art by Lucy Shaw from Creative Arts Charter School, and Kyle Chau and Sarah Knight-Weiss from Francisco Middle School. Photo of Ramona Arcega sitting on *Auspicious Clouds | Heavy Fog* by the artist, Michael Arcega.

Text design by Lynne Frost

Photo credits appear on pages 119–121

Library of Congress Cataloging-in-Publication Data

Names: Marshall, Julia, author. | Ledo-Lane, Ann, author. | McAvoy, Elizabeth, author.
Title: Integrating the visual arts across the curriculum : an elementary and middle school guide / Julia
    Marshall. With contributions by Ann Ledo-Lane and Elizabeth McAvoy.
Description: New York : Teachers College Press, [2019] | Includes bibliographical references and index.
Identifiers: LCCN 2019024288 (print) | LCCN 2019024289 (ebook) | ISBN 9780807761908 (paperback) |
    ISBN 9780807761915 (hardcover) | ISBN 9780807778012 (ebook)
Subjects: LCSH: Education, Elementary—Curricula. | Education, Secondary—Curricula. | Art—Study
    and teaching (Elementary) | Art—Study and teaching (Secondary) | Art in education.
Classification: LCC LB1570 .M366845 2019 (print) | LCC LB1570 (ebook) | DDC 372.5—dc23
LC record available at https://lccn.loc.gov/2019024288
LC ebook record available at https://lccn.loc.gov/2019024289

ISBN 978-0-8077-6190-8 (paper)
ISBN 978-0-8077-6191-5 (hardcover)
ISBN 978-0-8077-7801-2 (ebook)

Printed on acid-free paper
Manufactured in the United States of America

This book is dedicated to my husband Leonard, my son Douglas,
and my siblings Paul, Morley, Caroline, and Alan

Contents

Foreword

MY RECENT ENCOUNTERS with elementary and middle school students have included a discussion with a 9-year-old boy about different types of cargo ships, examining an 8-year-old boy's tiny, intricately detailed drawings of World War II-era military tanks, enjoying videos of how birds build nests with 7- to 10-year-olds, and hearing about how a 7-year-old's cardboard city had just suffered an imaginary explosion and killed the fish in the river. I talked to 3rd-graders about the losses suffered by Austrian Jews in the Holocaust by telling stories of confiscated paintings, and they told me their family stories. I have discussed the current global refugee crisis by showing how artist Erwin Wurm's *One Minute Sculptures* allow a viewer to interact with items a refugee might need. The students responded with empathy and care. These conversations show how young children are working with purposes similar to contemporary adult artists and art critics, who approach a topic with questions, curiosities, and concerns. They are positioning themselves within the community of artists who observe carefully, ask questions, form opinions, and make work that requires a viewer to look, think, and wonder. Julia Marshall's *Integrating the Visual Arts Across the Curriculum: An Elementary and Middle School Guide* is a resource for teachers who want to use those curiosities about the world to teach within an emergent curriculum, allowing inquiry to guide classroom practice and acknowledging that the meaning students gain from instruction will build upon itself over time. It provides academic structures and practical ideas for teachers to use as they oversee learning environments that encourage nonlinear, open-ended, and organic creative learning processes.

Marshall demonstrates how art making is a way to meaningfully engage with learning. Adult artists reference observations, elaborate on ideas, mimic the practices of other academic disciplines, satirize incongruities, and present new ways of viewing the world. As children learn through art and art play, they are looking, copying, elaborating, "poking fun," and engaging with the complexities of life. They employ both logical and associative thinking, utilizing form to convey content in the work. Marshall's view of arts integration challenges teaching practices based on knowledge acquisition through recall alone. She shows how the arts and math employ abstraction and an understanding of relationships and systems; how the arts and sciences use similar processes of observation, inquiry, and formation of theory; how the arts and writing convey information but also tell stories and acknowledge lived experience. She demonstrates how within different disciplines learning is a synthesis of observations, facts, experiences, and concepts acting as steps to evolving understandings. Finally, Marshall provides tools, strategies, and frameworks to develop curricula that align with how people think and learn.

Contemporary art is transdisciplinary, and arts integration in elementary and middle school art curricula can benefit from its practices. Within this book, Marshall provides educators with a well-researched resource bank of various contemporary artists that can be used in an elementary or middle school. I encourage the reader to look at the artists Marshall highlights as an introduction to each body of work and use them in the classroom. Conversations about contemporary artists allow students to apply learning from other subject areas to the art they are seeing, to talk about current events, and to tell their own stories. Children's responses to contemporary art are often similar to those of adults. They may initially respond with intrigue, confusion, or sometimes animosity to art that is different from what they have seen before. Then, through guided questioning, both children and adults examine clues to provide context, apply previous knowledge, develop opinions, discuss inconsistencies, critique forms, and find new questions for themselves. I see the resources in this book leading to rich and intriguing conversations as teachers study the artists that Marshall has chosen, prepare discussions, listen to kids, and value their opinions.

Marshall envisions teaching and learning as an inquiry trail. One fact, concept, question, or idea leads to another. Teachers can apply this metaphor as they plan learning experiences for their students. Students can make their own trails as they integrate content knowledge, contemporary art, and lived experience into art making. Marshall employs the term "poietic" to encompass the process of crafting something new, something conveying meaning through attention to form. The educational goal implied through the metaphor of inquiry trails and the description of poietic processes is that students will find their own paths, make new things, and find new ways to live within our common world.

If you long for an arts classroom that connects students to the astonishingly interesting world they live in and want some helpful guidance on how to do it, this is the book for you!

Connie Stewart
Professor of Art Education
School of Art and Design
University of Northern Colorado

Preface

THIS BOOK is about art integration and learning. It describes an approach to visual art integration inspired by practices in contemporary art and current ideas in education. In this approach, art making is understood to be a form of inquiry, and art integration, a practice that goes beyond simple illustration of academic subject matter to one that develops deeper understanding of subjects and how they work together as a whole. Here, art is the prime ingredient in creative inquiry—an approach that prompts young people to engage personally, actively, and deeply in their learning. The key to this approach to integration is creative thinking and connection making, which are inherent in all areas of inquiry but are highlighted in art.

The art-based inquiry approach I describe was developed over the years through research and practice with young people from kindergarten through elementary grades, middle school, high school, and university, and with classroom teachers. This work is highlighted in *Art-Centered Learning Across the Curriculum: Integrating Contemporary Art in the Secondary School Classroom,* which I coauthored with David Donahue (2014). Now, in this book, I want to introduce the approach to teachers in elementary and middle schools. While the approach is supported and guided by ideas from education, creativity theory, and contemporary art, its greatest value comes from listening to, experimenting with, and observing both learners and colleagues as they play with and apply their ideas. Their inspiration, ingenuity, and wisdom permeate the book.

In the spirit of its origins, this book connects theory to practice. It presents the concepts behind curriculum integration through creative art-based inquiry; provides strong, flexible frameworks and methods that teachers can use in their teaching; illustrates ways students can learn through contemporary art strategies and related pedagogy; and offers five models of inquiry trails that educators can adapt or pull from as they create, enhance, and grow their own art-based integrated curriculum. Because creative art-based inquiry finds inspiration and models in contemporary art, the book showcases relevant and child-friendly works of art. It does this in two ways: as examples of art that addresses key concepts in the academic disciplines, and as visual evidence of artists using creative strategies to make and convey meaning. "Keys to Understanding," special features that provide further information or thought-provoking questions to supplement the text narrative, appear throughout the book.

The book is organized into three parts. Part I covers the general rationale behind creative inquiry and integration. Part II discusses the four primary academic disciplines taught in schools—the natural sciences, mathematics, social studies, and language arts—with examples of related contemporary art. Part III provides frameworks and tools for curriculum development and implementation along with samples of integrated inquiry trails.

The book is intended to be a guidebook for implementing art-based creative inquiry and curriculum integration; it is not designed to be a one-method-fits-all formula. Instead, it provides a play structure and a map to support teachers in developing and deepening their own curriculum trails and to guide learners down those trails.

Acknowledgments

THIS BOOK owes its existence to the wisdom and support of many friends, colleagues, and members of my family. My deepest gratitude goes to my "home" editor, Leonard Hunter, who labored many hours over the original manuscript to make the text clearer and typo-free.

I especially thank two dedicated art educators whose work with young learners has contributed significantly to this volume. Ann Ledo-Lane, artist and Director of Arts Programming at the Creative Arts Charter School (CACS), San Francisco, California, was instrumental in the inquiry projects featured in Chapters 1 and 7, and has been an invaluable collaborator in developing this model of art integration for elementary school. Elizabeth McAvoy, who is exploring art-based inquiry in her art classes at Francisco Middle School in San Francisco, developed the scaffolding activities for independent art-based creative inquiry discussed in this book. Her students' work is also featured in Chapter 7.

I am grateful to Gina Griffiths and Ron Buchanan, who took their 1st-grade classes on a 3-month-long creative inquiry into their local community. They put an enormous amount of creativity, energy, and acumen into the activities documented in Chapter 1. Also, many thanks go to Grace Wilson and Katie Brinkley, 2nd-grade teachers at the CACS, who guided their students through the plant inquiry project illustrated in the research workbook section in Chapter 7.

I extend much gratitude to Kimberley D'Adamo, who has been my partner over the years in developing this approach. She has brilliantly adapted and grown art-based creative research practices in her high school art classes. Her ideas and those of her students permeate this book. I also want to give a shout out to the dedicated people who bring their smarts and passion to the ongoing development of creative integrated learning: Trena Noval, Louise Music, and the many teachers and teaching artists in the Alameda County Office of Education, Department of Integrated Learning.

A special thanks goes to David Donahue, my coauthor of *Art-Centered Learning Across the Curriculum* (2014), and to the collaborating authors of that volume: coauthors of Chapters 3, 5, and 8 Lawrence Horvath, Steven Drouin, and Ruth Cossey, and Rick Ayers, who wrote Chapter 7 of that book.

I am also deeply grateful to Susan Liddicoat, who painstakingly edited this book and made it "work." Her insights, guidance, and suggestions were invaluable. Also, I offer many thanks to Sarah Biondello, who guided this volume through the publication process; to Karl Nyberg, who also was very helpful; and to Lynne Frost, who designed the layout of the book, making it easy to read and visually engaging.

Lastly, I send many thanks to my dear friend Lisa Hochtritt, who first encouraged me to write this book and then cheered me on all the way.

PART I

Foundations of Creative Inquiry

IN PART I, I examine the foundations of the creative inquiry art-based approach to integration and learning. While Chapter 1 discusses the basic tenets of integrated learning within the context of a prolonged creative art-based inquiry project with 1st-graders, Chapter 2 provides the rationale behind curriculum integration as a way to enliven learning and build understanding of academic content. Art-based inquiry provides a creative lens and process through which to learn about, integrate, and make sense of what is taught in schools. With its juxtaposition of ideas to concrete examples, Part I sets the stage for exploring and connecting theory and practice in the chapters that follow.

1

Learning Through Creative Art-Based Inquiry

THERE ARE multiple forms of curriculum and many ways to teach. Which methods work better for young people? Which ones engage them both intellectually and emotionally? Which can tap into and build upon their natural inclinations and ways of being? One approach is to embed academic learning in an extensive thematic project that draws young learners into inquiry, discovery, and creation. This chapter explores *creative art-based inquiry,* an approach to teaching and learning particularly suited to youth that does all of this. I begin with an explanation of creative inquiry and all it entails, and then illustrate it with an example project trail from two 1st-grade classes at the Creative Arts Charter School (CACS) in San Francisco, California. Finally, I draw on this project to discuss other beneficial aspects of the creative inquiry approach.

The 1st-grade project at CACS was designed and led by the two 1st-grade teachers, Gina Griffiths and Ron Buchanan, with the guidance and support of arts specialist Ann Ledo-Lane. It was a 3-month exploration around the theme of "community." Under that thematic umbrella, the project trail covered a myriad of topics related to the academic curriculum, while connecting to the lives and interests of the students. When the 1st-graders began their exploration of community, they embarked on an art-based creative inquiry trail that included the following:

- Research excursions to explore and experience people, places, and activities related to their topic

- Answering and asking questions about all the information and ideas they encountered
- Creating artworks that conveyed their thinking

These are the hallmarks of creative inquiry, which is the artful engine of curriculum integration.

Our 1st-graders probably did not notice that they crossed over a few disciplinary boundaries as they explored their topics, articulated their ideas, and created their artworks. To them, this was not an exercise in arts integration in which they met social studies standards and language arts standards and honed their thinking skills, but an adventure into their neighborhood, their classroom community, and themselves.

CREATIVE ART-BASED INQUIRY LEARNING

This section discusses three kinds of inquiry-based learning beginning with the most rudimentary version of inquiry-based learning and moving on to art-based approaches to inquiry.

Inquiry-Based Learning

The term "inquiry" suggests a quest for knowledge that ventures into the unknown and is free-form and open-ended—like snooping around without a map, unsure of where the investigation will lead. In inquiry-based learning, however, the teacher has a general map of where the project can go and a set of benchmarks and goals. How the benchmarks are reached

FIGURE 1.1. Map of a Creative-Inquiry Trail

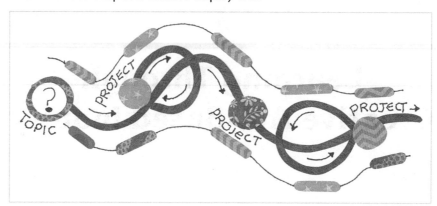

and goals achieved may be planned ahead, but the plan is also flexible and open-ended. That is to say, an inquiry-based approach to learning has a support structure and parameters, but allows for—even welcomes—spontaneity and the unexpected. When an unexpected turn arises, skillful teachers know how to embrace it, connect it to their goals, and fold it into the learning. Inquiry-based learning is emergent, meaning that it builds on itself and takes shape as it progresses. It advances through a series of interrelated steps in which learning is an exploration and an adventure into new territory. An apt metaphor for the trajectory of this mode of learning is a *trail*. On this trail, learners are trailblazers and teachers are their guides (see Figure 1.1).

A key trait of inquiry-based learning is its Constructivist approach to learning. This means that on an inquiry trail, knowledge is actively constructed by the learner rather than transmitted in advance by the teacher. Constructivist Learning Theory, which espouses this view of learning, has two primary concepts (Fosnot & Perry, 2005):

- Learners construct their own understandings as they interact with their environment (proposed by Piaget, 1955).
- Learning is the outcome of interpersonal interaction within a social, cultural, and historical context (proposed by Vygotsky, 2012).

Inquiry-based learning, with its teacher guidance, its hands-on, minds-on learning experiences, and its fostering of individual learning through social interaction, is Constructivist all the way.

KEYS TO UNDERSTANDING

The Principles of Constructivism

- Learners actively construct their own knowledge through interaction with the environment and with others.
- Emphasis is on cognitive development and deep understanding, rather than on behavior and development of skills.
- Reaching developmental stages is not simply the result of maturation but is understood as constructions achieved through active learner reorganization of knowledge.
- Learning is not a linear process but is complex and nonlinear.

Fosnot & Perry (2005)

What happens on an inquiry trail? The trail begins with a topic to explore and questions asked about the topic that stimulate learners' curiosity and launch their investigation. From there, students learn through study and experience. Their teacher encourages them to develop their own questions, ideas, and interpretations of information and experiences, and prompts them to think both critically and creatively. Each learning experience along the trail leads to the next experience, which, in turn, builds upon it and takes it further. This is a trail that proceeds step by step toward a goal. Along the way the teacher provides prompts and choices: assignments, hands-on activities, and reflection exercises that encourage learners to explore

---

KEYS TO UNDERSTANDING

The Tenets of Inquiry-Based Learning

- Learning is stimulated by inquiry—driven by questions or problems.
- Learning occurs during a process of constructing knowledge and new understandings.
- Inquiry-based learning is an active approach to learning that involves action and experience.
- Inquiry-based learning is a student-centered approach to teaching in which the teacher acts as facilitator.
- Inquiry-based learning progresses toward self-directed learning, with students taking increasing responsibility and control of their learning.
- The goal of inquiry is understanding.

Spronken-Smith & Walker (2010)

KEYS TO UNDERSTANDING

The Tenets of Creative Inquiry

- Creative thinking, making, and performing are key ways of learning. This includes multimodal applications and modes of learning.
- Subjectivity, personal interpretation, connection, and application are key to understanding and meaning making.
- Deeper understanding develops through realizing the implications of knowledge and information and building on them through extension, elaboration, and projection.
- Play and experimentation are critical to developing understanding and meaning.
- Creative inquiry is a creative learning process that moves forward in a meandering, nonlinear, and emergent way. It builds on itself as new "products" and outcomes arise and is thus open to interpretation and revision and to inspiring new thinking and creations.

---

ideas in personal ways and to build meaning and understanding for themselves.

Creative Inquiry and Learning

All inquiry has its creative aspects. The connection making and problem solving that take place in any inquiry-based learning are creative in the way they entail finding likenesses, making inferences, and applying information. *Creative inquiry,* however, embraces the more adventuresome creativity of experimental and imaginative play with ideas and possibilities. This play, which generates imaginative leaps, fresh perspectives, and unexpected connections, is a primary method of learning in creative inquiry.

How do creative play and imagination generate learning? John Dewey (1902) argued that a child learns by applying information to a task. That is, learning occurs when information is engaged or applied. Generic inquiry-based learning is laced with activities in which information or knowledge is applied, theorized, and represented. When these activities are *creative,* as in creative inquiry, information is applied imaginatively. The learner uses information to formulate something new, to make new inferences, or to approach something from a fresh vantage point. In doing so, learning is amplified because, in a creative endeavor, a learner not

only applies what she is learning but also plays with its possibilities. To do so, a learner must analyze information, distill it down, and find its salient features. That is, imaginative application requires a learner to have some grasp of the information before leaping forward with it. Creative inquiry takes full advantage of the power of imagination and play. It is a quest for understanding shaped and propelled by creative processes and hands-on making.

The nonlinear path of creative processes contributes to creativity's capacity to enhance and advance learning. It allows the learner to play, experiment, and try out ideas, and its open-ended nature encourages learning to expand and branch off in organic, often messy and surprising ways. While this is also a trait of standard inquiry-based learning, the tendency to roam and branch is amplified in creative inquiry.

Creative inquiry also spirals as it moves toward an outcome. Cycling around in spirals entails revisiting ideas and information, reinterpreting them, and, possibly, revising one's perspective. Multiple, deeper, more complex understandings of the topic can emerge. This phenomenon is amplified when art making is part of the process—when creative inquiry becomes *art-based creative inquiry*. Why is that? The artworks created along the way provide resource material for the next step of inquiry. Learners can mine their artworks for information and ideas embedded in them. In this way, students can learn from what they have created.

Ultimately, the cyclical/spiral nature of creative inquiry shows students the following:

- Learning is organic, following a trail that leads naturally from one thing to another.
- Learning is emergent, building on itself.
- Knowledge is never set, but is flexible and open to revision.
- Learning is a personal construction built through experience, creation, and reflection (see Figure 1.2).

Art-Based Creative Inquiry: Contributions from Contemporary Art

Art-based creative inquiry applies contemporary artists' ideas, ways of thinking, and studio practices to learning. Its purpose is twofold:

- To help learners develop the habits, dispositions, and thinking skills artists use to understand and convey their ideas
- To open up learning to imagination and play, thus giving learners freedom from conventional academic constraints to take ideas further

Artists model creative inquiry in the ways they think and explore, and in the forms and creative strategies they use to present their ideas. Regarding thinking, artists are known for approaching problems, ideas, or topics from multiple, often eccentric and playful perspectives; they are lauded for how they think in nonlinear ways and make unexpected connections. They are also known for crystallizing complex ideas into powerfully simple forms or for doing the opposite: bringing complexity to something that is seemingly simple.

The process of making art *is* creative inquiry—an iterative, emergent practice of exploration and experimentation through the medium of artworks. Artists present their ideas and interpretations in forms that give shape to things that are otherwise invisible, abstract, and inaccessible. These forms are aesthetic; they engage viewers both emotionally and intellectually. Visual artists draw a viewer in with the lyricism of design, form, color, movement, pattern, texture, line, and space, and their human touch makes the ideas they address come alive.

Beyond this, contemporary artists use *creative strategies* in devising artworks. These strategies are deceptively simple methods for conveying complex ideas, provoking thought, or jump starting a creative inquiry. Educators can employ these strategies when they design curriculum to bring creative learning into the mix, as I discuss further in Chapter 7. Learners can also employ the strategies to bring new twists to subjects or make their learning more personal and enjoyable. It is important to note that many of these art strategies come naturally to children and young people—particularly elaborating, personifying, drawing analogy/metaphor, projecting, and embodying/play acting. Many of these strategies are at play in all the arts but find their apotheosis in storytelling.

Role of the Teacher

In creative inquiry-based learning, the teacher is a guide whose task it is to *provoke* (jump start the inquiry with an activity and/or questions), *enable* (provide just enough information, scaffolding, and guidance to facilitate students' progress down the path), and *allow* (let learners run with information and ideas, and make them their own). Together the three pillars of creative inquiry pedagogy—provoke, enable, and allow—provide a structure that is

- Stimulating enough to generate profound thinking and push learners to go deeply into what a body of knowledge means and why it is important
- Strong enough to support and guide learners' inquiry
- Flexible enough to embrace tangents, surprises, personal interpretations, and creativity

FIGURE 1.2. Map of the Recursive Process of Creative Inquiry

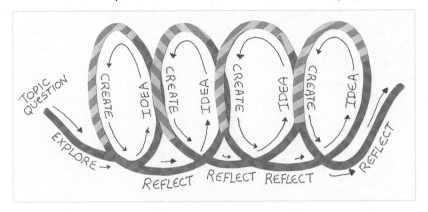

Guidelines for achieving a balance among structure, rigor, and freedom in creative inquiry are provided in Chapters 7 and 8 of this book.

THE FIRST-GRADE COMMUNITY INQUIRY

Introduced earlier, the 1st-graders' community project trail at the Creative Arts Charter School shows all the earmarks of creative inquiry in action. We see this in its extended, recursive process; in its mix of hands-on and minds-on activities; and in the creative art strategies the children employed. The project began with initial questions and thinking about the overarching concept of community, thus tapping into students' prior knowledge and understanding of the concept. This early thinking took place as the children mapped and constructed a miniature model of a neighborhood (see Figure 1.3). Their work illustrates how envisioning and mapping reveal learners' understanding through visual/physical forms and presence.

From there, the trail progressed to excursions into the neighborhood. These outings gave the children opportunities to explore how the abstract notion of community plays out in specific examples in real life, thus deepening their preliminary understandings of the concept. The excursions included walking in the neighborhood with sketchpads while observing and drawing various styles of architecture, as well as visiting a variety of businesses and services, such as the bakery, the coffee shop, the veterinary clinic, and the fire station. In these places, the children were able to see "neighborhood helpers" at work and talk to them about what they do.

In this lively way, the adult world opened up to the children. The neighborhood helpers told stories about life at their work, invited the children to look behind the scenes, gave them opportunities to pretend they were workers or customers, and provided them with direct experiences of the sites. For example, at the veterinary clinic, the children each listened to the beating heart of a dog; at the bakery, they made and ate giant pretzels; at the coffee house, they learned about how espresso machines steam milk; and at the firehouse, they watched a fireman demonstrate how to slide down the fire pole. The salient lessons that emerged from these encounters were about how much goes into doing a job well; how much each neighborhood helper contributes in his or her own way to the community at

FIGURE 1.3. Model Showing Learners' Initial Thinking About the Idea of Community

FIGURE 1.4. Recording How Students Used the Studio Habits of Mind

FIGURE 1.5. Imitating Buildings

FIGURE 1.6. Exploring and Learning Through Mapping

large; and how jobs can be the source of enjoyment, and in many cases, a passion to those who perform them.

These rich and varied explorations were viewed through the Studio Habits of Mind (Hetland, Winner, Veneema, & Sheridan, 2013) (Figure 1.4) and integrated with numerous art-based activities, such as the following:

- Imitating buildings with their bodies to get a sense of the parts of buildings and their structures and functions (Figure 1.5)
- Examining the elements and purposes of maps and then drawing their own maps of their neighborhood (Figure 1.6)
- Drawing self-portraits as their chosen neighborhood helpers (see Figure 1.7)

- Writing and illustrating books about their neighborhood helpers and their stories (see Figure 1.8)

These activities and explorations provided an abundance of information and ideas for the next steps of the trail. While the project could have proceeded in a variety of ways, teachers Gina Griffiths and Ron Buchanan and art specialist Ann Ledo-Lane took it in a decidedly artistic direction when they asked each child to choose a building from the neighborhood to represent him or her. Here the teachers introduced the creative art strategy of *metaphor* in 1st-grade terms and invited each child to enter into a sequence of complex thinking and connection making that involved assessing his or her personality, talents, and aspirations, and then to designate a building that best embodies them.

FIGURE 1.7. Zita Vitola-Giorni, Self-Portrait as a Neighborhood Helper

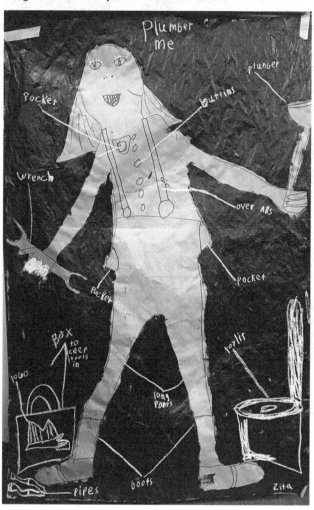

FIGURE 1.8. Vita Cuellar, Juniper Ximm, Adeline Foster, and Angelo Barillas, Illustrated Books About Neighborhood Helpers

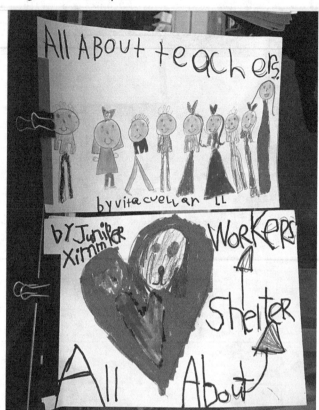

Making the metaphorical connection was not difficult for most of the children. However, to be sure they all understood, Gina facilitated their metaphorical thinking by doing some of her own: She described herself as a flower shop. Gina told the children that she chose a flower shop because she wants everyone to think of flowers when they see her. She then asked her students to think about what they like to do, what they are like, and how they would like to be seen.

From there, the class listed the kinds of buildings they encountered on their tours of the neighborhood, and each child chose the building with which he or she felt kinship. It was a small step from there to draw their metaphorical buildings and construct them out of paper and cardboard. Figure 1.9 is Luma's drawing of his metaphorical building. Since his father is a firefighter, choosing a firehouse for his metaphor came naturally to Luma. The import of selecting this metaphor goes further, however. Luma expressed how he sees himself as a helper, and this allowed him to designate a set of traits he wants to cultivate and be known for (see also Figure 1.10). Another student, Griffin, elected to see himself as Sutro Tower, a gigantic jungle gym-style microwave tower in the center of San Francisco. He explained, "I am Sutro Tower. I like to charge things up. I'm a charged-up kid."

After constructing their buildings, the children were ready to plot their community and, thereby, stretch the metaphor. For this, they designed a network of streets on which to place their buildings. While, on one level, this web of streets stood as a physical representation of their neighborhood, it also performed in a subtler way as a metaphor for the children's connections to each other (see Figure 1.11).

FIGURE 1.9. Luma Ayish, "I Would Be the Fire House . . . I Am a Helper"

Taking the metaphorical leap was key to reaching the potential of the entire project trail. It not only prompted the children to take their thinking in a more imaginative direction, but it also enhanced the personal meaning of what they were doing and learning. While the metaphorical expressions tied the project all together, the other creative strategies—such as mapping, embodying, and storytelling—were key elements as well. These strategies surrounded the core metaphors of buildings and streets with rich layers of information, experiences, and ideas. They were the strategies that allowed the project to soar—to make the trail climb higher.

OTHER KEY ASPECTS OF THE CREATIVE INQUIRY APPROACH

Earlier in this chapter, I explained the basics of the creative inquiry approach. In the following I draw on the 1st-graders' experiences in their community project trail to discuss some other important traits and benefits of creative inquiry.

Mix of Associative and Logical Thinking

When we examine the kinds of thinking the 1st-graders employed in their work, we find they analyzed,

FIGURE 1.10. Luma Ayish, Firehouse

FIGURE 1.11. The Streets That Connect Us

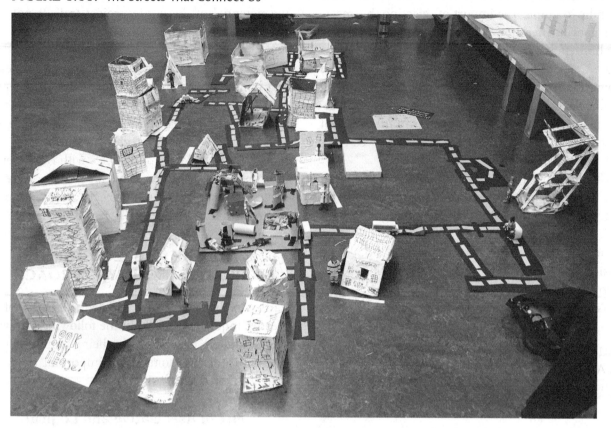

synthesized, and came to logical conclusions on the one hand, and envisioned, imagined, and made unusual connections on the other. In doing so, they engaged in a complex kind of thinking that fuels all creative endeavors: *poietic logic.* Poietic logic is a combination of logical, linear thinking (reason) and associative, creative thinking (imagination). The word "poietic" comes from the Greek *poiesis,* to create or make. As the counterpoint to mimesis, which for the ancient Greeks meant to reenact or repeat, *poiesis* is associated with processes of creating something new (Trueit, 2005).

Poietic logic, the mix of two contrasting kinds of thinking, drives the quest for knowledge in all domains, but it is particularly prominent in the arts and art-based creative inquiry. It is the kind of thinking practitioners use to break new ground, invent new things, and find possibilities and poetry in whatever they explore. It is important to underscore here that creative inquiry and art making require a *balance* of logic and imagination. This balance is particularly important when it comes to learning.

FIGURE 1.12. Map of the Cycle of Knowledge Construction

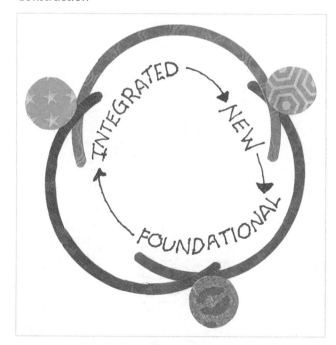

Why is balance important? On the one hand, reasoning and logic, both rudiments of critical thinking, are crucial to deciphering the real world and figuring things out. Examining reality in thoughtful and deep ways is not only essential for education, it is important as a foundation for making imaginative statements that elucidate reality—the very kind of statements we often see in art. Indeed, critical thinking sets the stage for creative thinking and frequently occurs in tandem with it. That is, artists and learners involved in creative production think critically and logically as they think creatively. Linear thinking and logic are important strands in the creative process; one cannot construct an object in space, mix just the right color, compose an image, convey a message, or realize a metaphor without some logical thinking (Efland, 2002). On the other hand, too much logical linear thinking can be counterproductive both in learning and in art making. It can overpower creative thinking, and when it does, the art and the learning do not deepen or soar beyond the literal to reach their potential.

Knowledge in Creative Inquiry

In creative inquiry, knowledge and creativity are intricately linked. This becomes most apparent when we identify the three kinds of knowledge learners tap into and construct on their inquiry trails. Fink (2013) identified two kinds of knowledge: foundational and integrated. For our inquiry trail, to Fink's list of foundational and integrated knowledge a third category can be added to accommodate creativity: new knowledge. Thus, I focus on three kinds of knowledge:

- *Foundational knowledge,* which includes academic knowledge and the funds of knowledge children bring to school from their lives and experiences
- *Integrated knowledge,* an understanding of how different aspects of foundational knowledge fit together and the significant underlying ideas that connect them
- *New knowledge,* the knowledge learners construct from the first two forms of knowledge

New knowledge includes learners' subjective interpretations of information and ideas, as well as

their inventions, visions, and other applications of knowledge. Learners begin with foundational knowledge; next they analyze that knowledge to connect it and integrate it; from there, learners take this integrated knowledge and apply it, expand from it, or invent something new from it (new knowledge). The new knowledge then becomes part of the foundational knowledge for the next learning cycle (see Figure 1.12).

It is important to note that all three types of knowledge are indispensable to the creative inquiry process. Because foundational knowledge provides the substance for the other two kinds of knowledge, the broader, deeper, and more abundant it is, the more creative and meaningful are the integrated knowledge and the new knowledge that arise from it. Designating the three kinds of knowledge is vital to understanding the workings of creative inquiry because it highlights the importance of a broad foundation of information and ideas for creativity, while it simultaneously emphasizes creative thinking, fantasy, and invention as equally valuable contributors to building foundational and integrated knowledge.

Dispositions Toward Learning

One of the more consequential benefits of creative inquiry is how it enables learners to dig into academic knowledge and meet academic standards in ways that come naturally to children. As mentioned earlier, children learn through activities such as questioning and experimenting, following their curiosities, making things, pretending, elaborating, and embellishing through storytelling. It follows that creative activities, which incorporate these child-friendly modes, are particularly important to cultivating positive dispositions for learning:

- Motivation to learn
- A sense of personal agency and independence
- Flexibility in thinking and applying information
- Resiliency in the face of disappointment or challenge
- The ability to embrace ambiguity and uncertainty

Engaging in creative activities also encourages young people's innate openness to new ideas, situations, and things. Each child is endowed with these dispositions or is capable of developing them. Doing creative inquiry is one way to ensure that these dispositions are not diminished as children grow up, but are instead firmly established for a lifetime of intellectual growth and learning.

Metacognition

A learner's positive attitude toward learning can also be a matter of understanding how learning occurs. Metacognition, the ability to understand and monitor one's own learning (Kolencik & Hillwig, 2011; Silver, 2013), is considered a must for academic success and a contributor to a learner's emotional well-being. Kolencik and Hillwig (2011) stress how metacognition helps learners to develop positive dispositions toward learning, particularly since it enables learners to improve their learning and take control. Metacognition, therefore, is key to navigating challenges and problems, and fulfilling one's potential. It is important to note that metacognition develops over time, and it can be activated and nurtured in the lower grades.

Metacognition requires stepping back from a task to name and frame what happens within it (Silver, 2013). Creative art-based inquiry provides an ideal setting for developing metacognition because it entails many kinds of thinking and doing, which are open to continual examination. When children are encouraged to step back—to reflect and elaborate on what they are doing and to assess the artifacts of learning they create—their attention is drawn toward the process of learning itself. Thus, metacognition materializes. Educators can help this process along by asking guiding reflection questions that prompt children to think about their thinking (see Chapter 8) and by conducting group discussions in which children go beyond talking about *what* they learned to discussing *how* they learned.

To develop metacognition, it is important to make reflection on thinking and learning a recurring, ongoing activity and to do it in a variety of ways. This can be by direct means such as writing and dialogue, or it can be accomplished through more creative art-based

FIGURE 1.13. Raul's Maps of the Brain (**A**) Learning (Connecting) and (**B**) Not Learning (Not Connecting)

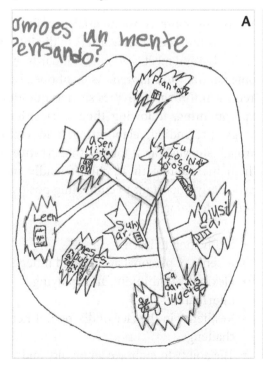

methods such as mapping the process, making art images that represent learning, or extending projects to surround the initial art "products" in more artworks that illustrate the thinking that went into those previous works (see Chapter 9 for ideas).

Figure 1.13 is a map, an art-based way to represent understanding of how learning works. It shows a 6-year-old's pictures of what happens when his brain is learning and when it is not learning. Raul, a student in Linsey Weizenberg Larimore's 1st-grade class at Glen Park Elementary School in San Francisco, made these maps after his class discussed how learning occurs when students connect something they are learning about to something they knew before.

Raul employed metaphors of a brain compartmentalized (no learning) and a brain with connected parts (learning) to describe how his learning works and then drew his metaphors to make them visible. In doing so, he built understanding of learning and then demon-strated his understanding of it. *Making learning visible* is key to developing metacognition, particularly when the subject illustrated and chronicled is thinking and/or learning. Chapter 8 of this book discusses Project Zero's Making Learning Visible Framework (Krechevsky, Mardell, Rivard, & Wilson, 2013) and its methods for fostering thinking, learning, and metacognition in all domains. The learning walls of the 1st-grade community project trail are an example of how the Making Learning Visible Framework can tie the disparate parts of a project trail together, reveal the rationale behind the project, highlight the learning and thinking that took place, and help learners to become metacognitive.

FROM THIS chapter's exploration of creative inquiry and its benefits, I move on to discussing one of its primary outcomes: curriculum integration.

2

Curriculum Integration Through Creative Inquiry

WHAT IS curriculum integration? Why is it important? How can we integrate the curriculum? What does art have to do with it? This chapter explores these questions. I begin by discussing how the academic disciplines work together in a system. I then look at curriculum integration, its benefits to learners, and different ways it can be done. I end by discussing visual art, its integrative nature, and its many functions in integration and learning.

THE DISCIPLINES: OVERLAPS, INTERSECTIONS, AND HYBRIDS

Schools, even at the elementary level, often teach subjects separately. Discrete time slots are designated for language arts, math, science, and social studies, and each discipline is explored independently during the day. This division of the curriculum honors the specific contributions and knowledge of each area of inquiry, and it is important for learners to dive deeply into each discipline and its specialized knowledge to understand it more fully. For that reason, isolated study of disciplines has merit (Beane, 2011). On the flip side, however, a "silo" approach to curriculum, which strictly divides the school day into discipline-based segments, implies that the various disciplines are completely separate. This is problematic because, outside of school, real-world problems are not limited to one discipline's knowledge or problem-solving methods. Each problem spills over disciplinary lines, requiring multiple ways of researching, thinking about, and solving it (Beane, 2011; Clark, 1997).

The disciplines also overlap in ways beyond problem solving. For example, the natural sciences share a common purpose with the social sciences: to understand our world and ourselves within it. Both focus on concepts and patterns underlying phenomena. Both find that their specific subjects are also covered in part by the other field. Both inquire into phenomena using similar thinking and processes.

Math is connected to the natural and social sciences because it allows for quantitative measurement and clear, concise recounting of factors in studies and the results of those studies. Math also enables scientists to construct mathematical models to make predictions. Math and language arts share common ground as well; both involve symbol systems that enable us to think concretely and abstractly and to communicate ideas and information. Language arts—verbal and written language—permeate every discipline, enabling specialists to articulate what they find, what they think, and what it could mean.

Furthermore, many disciplines coalesce to create hybrid disciplines. These hybrids are domains that bridge territory between the traditional disciplines, using methods and ideas from their component disciplines to study specific phenomena. Ecology, for instance, combines the social and natural sciences to grasp how people interact with and affect the natural environment, while it uses math for calculations and statistical analysis, cartography to see locations and trends, and stories to make abstract findings about the environment real and palpable. Geography, economics, and archaeology are also hybrid domains.

With all the overlap, interaction, and merging of disciplines in the real world, the separation of disciplines in an educational or research setting is certainly artificial, but it is also expedient and necessary (Beane, 2011). The pursuit of knowledge is divided into disciplines for a good reason: Practitioners can specialize and concentrate on subjects, enabling them to go into detail and allowing them to do it in the most appropriate ways. But this specialization, of course, means that researchers might miss something because they are too close to their subject or are locked into discipline-specific conventions and practices. Taking a wider view—stepping outside for a moment to see something from a different vantage point—can help. That is why a broad vision (or an integrated picture) is important. It balances details with the whole, contextualizes them, and allows for new perspectives to arise (Clark, 1997; Gnanakan, 2011).

Despite their differences, the disciplines fit together as a *system* (Clark, 1997). Fleener (2005) defines a system as a complex structure composed of multiple interrelated parts that is dynamic, evolving, and adapts to its environment. A systems perspective enables us to see the disciplines as collaborative, interactive, and always evolving. A good metaphor for this system is an animal cell. Why? A cell is a living system composed of parts that work together, each with its own role and mechanisms, and each vital to the well-being of the whole.

CURRICULUM INTEGRATION

Integration emphasizes cross-disciplinary connections. These connections become visible and accessible through investigation of a topic from multiple angles through the lens of several disciplines and connecting the topic to related information and ideas from broad areas of knowledge.

Integration is, metaphorically speaking, a spiderweb. A spiderweb illustrates how curriculum integration is an intricate network of connections centered around a topic. The concentric circles of the web radiate out from the core and are laced together by threads

> ### KEYS TO UNDERSTANDING
>
> #### Purposes of Curriculum Integration
>
> - To help learners build deep and broad understandings of academic content and its relationship to their lives.
> - To make academic content cohere so it has meaning, thus motivating learners to learn about it and make sense of it.
> - To underscore how all disciplines are areas of inquiry in which knowledge is interconnected and always evolving.
> - To foreground meaning and understanding.

that span among them. While the web represents curriculum connections, it also implies the purpose of curriculum integration: to put a topic in context to build complex understanding of it. David Perkins (1988) helps us draw a direct connection between integration and understanding through his description of *understanding* as a web. He sees understanding as a matter of placing something within its "web of associations that give it meaning" (p. 113). Curriculum integration corresponds with Perkins's web metaphor in highlighting connections. His web metaphor also suggests how understanding is similar to integration in the way it centers around a hub: the topic.

Substantive Multidimensional Integration

Understanding requires going beyond superficial connections to search for hidden connections and big transdisciplinary ideas or concepts. It also calls for making procedural connections—identifying how various disciplines are similar in their practices and often borrow methods from other disciplines. I describe this integration as both *substantive* because it connects specific knowledge to "Big Ideas" (concepts) and addresses significant issues, and *multidimensional* because it does so in multiple ways—both discipline-specific and interdisciplinary. We can examine this approach to integration through the lens of Boix-Mansilla and Gardner's (1998) Four Dimensions of

Understanding: purpose, knowledge, methods, and forms. In the explanation that follows, the methods and forms are merged.

Purpose. Why engage in substantive multidimensional curriculum integration? Substantive multidimensional curriculum integration has two complementary goals. First, it enables learners to see the complexity of ideas and information. This means looking at many facets of a topic or idea to understand it more fully. This happens when learners "spin" a complex web of understanding that spans disciplines. Second, it makes things simpler by placing topics and ideas within a cohesive vision. This enables learners to see why these things matter and how they fit into the whole. It also helps young people learn and remember better because learning is not mired in detail but, instead, is focused on ideas, meaning, and understanding.

Knowledge. The knowledge of curriculum integration encompasses the three kinds of knowledge discussed in Chapter 1: *foundational, integrated,* and *new* knowledge. Although integration highlights integrated knowledge, this knowledge is one of three parts of a cycle. Foundational knowledge forms the necessary underpinning of integrated knowledge, and conversely, integrated knowledge is the result of synthesis and understanding of foundational knowledge. Integrated knowledge also provides a stepping stone toward new knowledge since learners create their own (i.e., new) knowledge from integration's synthesis of information and ideas that span the disciplines.

Methods and Forms. What pedagogy can we use to integrate curriculum? Following are three closely related approaches to integrating the curriculum: project-based, inquiry-based, and creative inquiry-based learning.

Project-Based Learning. Projects are a popular pedagogical method for integration. A project is a purposeful activity or series of connected activities in which learners actively use questions to explore and tackle significant problems, issues, and concerns posed by life (Beane, 2011; Hunter-Koniger, 2018). While the significance of a project topic is one key to

a meaningful project, the way the topic is approached is equally important. In a project, learners do not simply identify questions and concerns, receive answers, and go no further; they put knowledge to work. When they do this, the knowledge learners apply or study has more meaning and is more likely to be learned and remembered. Furthermore, because these issues or problems are important to the learner and the world, and because learners actively participate in solving them, the learner is more highly motivated to learn and engage. All in all, integrated learning projects provide a viable alternative to passive or rote learning (Beane, 2011).

Not all projects, however, count as integrative projects. Beane's concept of a project stands in stark contrast to artificial academic puzzles or exercises that are discipline-specific and disconnected from reality. In an art curriculum, for example, lessons or units frequently are called "projects," but they are not the kinds of projects that Beane envisions since they are often focused on discipline-specific ideas and skills and are sequenced as discrete lessons. They may have some of the attributes of Beane's version of project-based learning, such as active, hands-on learning and problem-solving, but they do not connect to the all-important requirement of investigating topics outside of the art domain.

Inquiry-Based Learning. Inquiry-based learning provides a broader notion of "project" than either Beane's or art classes' versions of project-based learning. In inquiry-based learning, the "project" is not a discrete entity but a sustained inquiry with sequential projects that link up under the umbrella of inquiry. We see this in the 1st-grade exploration of community in Chapter 1, where various projects or learning experiences are located along an inquiry trail. While each project integrates in its own way, the inquiry trail, and the investigation that propels it, are the binding agents of curriculum integration. They link projects together to give these activities coherence and connection, momentum, and direction, by placing them within the broader context of a learning continuum. As they blaze their trail, learners spin webs of association (Perkins, 1988) and generate multiple connections to Big Ideas. Walking the trail and spinning the webs along it generate integration, and learners do it in an organic, iterative, ever-evolving, multileveled, and purposeful way.

Creative Inquiry-Based Learning. Creative inquiry is discussed in Chapter 1. Briefly, creative inquiry-based integration allows young people to learn by imaginatively interpreting and re-visioning school content and inventing something new from it. Creative inquiry links Perkins's (1988) theory of understanding to creativity. In creative inquiry, learners play with ideas and information in imaginative ways. They come to understand topics through creative thinking and making. Creative inquiry, therefore, is creativity for understanding.

Creativity in and Through Integration

Why is curriculum integration a source of and medium for creativity? Connection making is a basic trait of creative thinking (Finke, Ward, & Smith, 1996). It follows that curriculum integration, through pushing on disciplinary boundaries and identifying webs of connection, is creative by its very nature and thus promotes creativity in learning. Through crossing borders, integration presents a merging or collision of ideas and information that propels learners to make new and oblique associations that surprise and generate fresh ideas and perspectives. This is similar to how cutting-edge transdisciplinary and hybrid disciplines in the adult professional world foment new, associative, and inventive thinking (Fleener, 2005).

Curriculum integration also enables learners to invent new methods for making connections and building webs of understanding. It brings the tools of inquiry from all the disciplines into the toolbox, and it encourages hybridizing those tools to create new tools. Furthermore, it also encourages creative thinking and drawing on themes and information from multiple disciplines in unorthodox ways. This allows for multiple ways to do creative inquiry.

ART AS AN INTEGRATIVE DISCIPLINE

How is integration a natural fit for contemporary art? The answers to this question lie in the nature of art today. Over the centuries and across the globe, art has had its various themes, conventions, and forms that expressed the values and preoccupations of a particular time and place. Today's art follows in that tradition; it is all about now. In the spirit of today's global, high-tech world, art explores everything that concerns us today, whether it be social, cultural, environmental, or personal. It also borrows from and crosses over into popular culture. That is to say, art is eclectic and free in what it chooses to tackle.

Moreover, current art reflects our time in the way it has broken with many of the conventional methods and forms of the past. Art is no longer a domain with mandatory baseline skills most commonly taught in schools; it is not limited to the tools and methods of art used in time-honored art and craft forms such as painting, drawing, printmaking, sculpture, textiles, photography, jewelry, and ceramics. Today, digital arts, performance art, interventionist art, animation, video, web art, and collaborative and community art have expanded the realm and methods of art. While contemporary art is adventuresome in its use of "non-art" methods and forms, it also stretches the boundaries of art and often defies categorization.

Because contemporary art is less concerned with being "art" in the conventional sense, but more about aesthetic experience, ideas, and meaning making, art is at liberty to be what it is: a free-wheeling creative lens on academic topics. Contemporary art, then, is a practice in which meaning making is not burdened with conventional rules, boundaries, and expectations either of the academic disciplines or of traditional art practices.

Furthermore, today's art is integrative in its stance. Artists often see a bigger or a different picture than the practitioners who deal with the details and procedures of an academic discipline. This means artists can be critics and cutups; they can see issues and ideas from an outside vantage point and are able to explore an issue freely. Because of this, they are able to poke fun or "make trouble." All of the above (eclectic subject matter, experimental methods, and outsider vantage point) make art far more powerful and relevant to today's world and to young people.

Contemporary art's proclivity to cross boundaries and invent new forms may cause viewers to wonder whether a work is art or not. One might ask, "Is it art?" That, however, is no longer the question. "What does it mean?" is now the question. This focus on meaning making dovetails with the conceptual basis of most contemporary art. Art today is about ideas, and ideas are the outcome and fodder of thinking. Therefore, contemporary art is about ideas, thinking, and meaning making. This troika of attributes makes contemporary art particularly suited to learning and integration. This means that current art—in contrast to the art most often taught in schools, with its traditional genres, forms, and sets of techniques—is more compatible with the goals of schools than its predecessors were. Still, art is most often taught as a solitary discipline focused on traditional art conventions. This can cause trouble for art as an educational discipline: It can be devalued and marginalized, and this can lead to its elimination. It also should be noted that art no longer must be taught separately to maintain its allegiance to the discipline of art. Indeed, if art is siloed as a narrow and distinct discipline in schools, it is not up to date with contemporary professional art practices.

Furthermore, separating art presents a lost opportunity for schools. When art is engaged as a way to learn and make meaning, it can transform schools and learning. Just as contemporary art seeks to turn things upside down or go deeper in the outside world, art can do the same for learners and schools.

How does art prompt thinking, ideation, and meaning making in learning? Art asks important questions and prompts learners to do the same. Art also does not explicitly answer questions but provokes learners to think. Art can be complex and ambiguous, which, like a puzzle, entices learners to ponder and wonder (see Figure 2.1, Timea Tihanyi's *Cosmology for a Skeptic* [2015]). Art also disrupts conventional ways of thinking, prompting a learner to question perception (see Figure 2.2, Jane Hammond's *My Heavens* [2004]). Furthermore, art can show how art ideas are born when the strategy used to make meaning is so upfront and visible (see Figure 2.3, Justin Lee's *Warrior* [ND]). (These three works are discussed further in Chapter 7.)

Why is art innately integrative? Contemporary artists often play with ideas and methods from non-art disciplines. Much contemporary art is inventive, insightful, and meaningful because it explores Big Ideas through specific topics associated with other areas of inquiry and also uses methods and materials from those domains. It should be noted that inspiration from outside of art is not a contemporary phenomenon or one limited to artists who "integrate." With the possible exception of minimalism, formalism, or pure abstraction, all artists get their ideas and topics from life.

In the past, the subjects of art have been connected to history and social studies. Historical figures and events are time-honored staples of the visual arts in most cultures. The same goes for social groups and culture. We see this universally in family portraits and depictions of everyday life. Likewise, art has always had a deep connection to nature, with its studies of natural phenomena. Examples are Chinese, Japanese, and Korean nature studies; European bestiaries; and natural history illustration. Indeed, the primary purpose of art has always been interpreting, understanding the world, reinforcing cultural norms or political power, or even changing them—and not about art styles, techniques, or genres.

Moreover, the tools and methods of science have been applied in the visual arts for a long time—from Italian Renaissance artists, such as Masaccio, who applied geometry to develop one-point perspective in naturalistic paintings, and Leonardo Da Vinci, whose scientific and engineering work informed his artwork; to the 17th-century natural history artists, who employed magnifying glasses, telescopes, and field-study books in their art; to 18th-century painters such as Canaletto, who used the camera obscura to help them render realistic pictures of spaces. Thus, scientific tools advanced art.

Contemporary art follows in this tradition of using new technologies to extend its reach into invisible worlds. As it does, art calls attention to the affiliation of art and science and takes art into realms of perception that advanced technology has opened up to us. For example, photographer Catherine Wagner uses magnetic resonance imaging (MRI) machines to capture images of the interior structures of fruits and vegetables.

Contemporary art also shifts art's focus away from exploring standard subjects of art, such as nature or perceptions of the world, toward the disciplinary practices of science. We see this in the artwork of Hine

FIGURE 2.1. Timea Tihanyi, *Cosmology for a Skeptic* (2015)

FIGURE 2.3. Justin Lee, *Warrior* (ND)

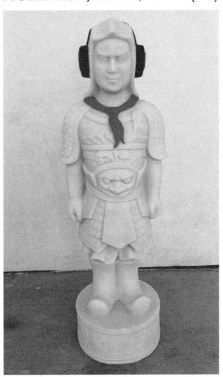

FIGURE 2.2. Jane Hammond, *My Heavens* (2004)

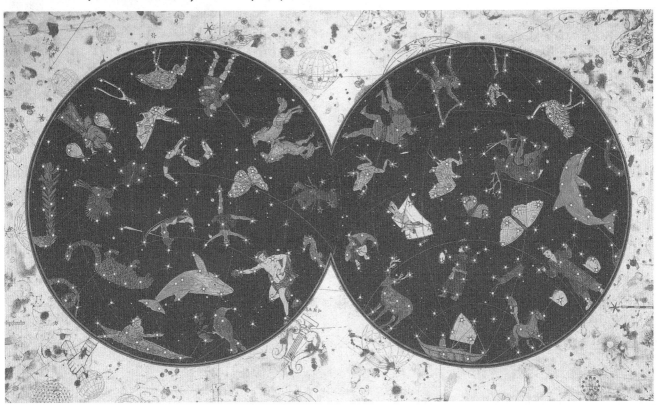

FIGURE 2.4. Hine Mizushima, *Unnatural History Museum (Giant Daphnias)* (ND)

FIGURE 2.5. Hine Mizushima, *Unnatural History Museum (Giant Paramecium)* (ND)

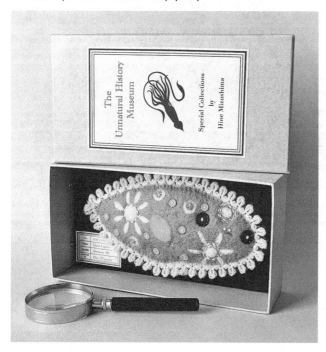

Mizushima (see Figures 2.4 and 2.5; see also Chapter 3), Mark Dion, Walmoor Correa, Hyung Koo Lee, and Amy Franceschini, who utilize basic scientific tools, such as microscopes and magnifying glasses, and traditional scientific display formats. In using these older forms and methods of the sciences, these artists highlight the basic ways we think about the natural and social worlds and how our thinking has been shaped

FIGURE 2.6. Maria Penil Cobo in collaboration with Mehmet Berkman, *Brain Matter* (2018)

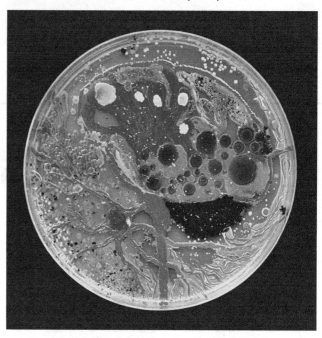

FIGURE 2.7. Amy Youngs, *Cute Parasites* (2008)

by the ways scientists have researched, interpreted, and presented the world to us.

The integration of art and science reaches its apotheosis when new art forms emerge. One of the more radical (and often disturbing) new art forms to come out of the science/art nexus is Bio Art—art that "manipulates the processes of life" (Kac, 2007, p. 18), using living organisms as its "materials" and living processes as part of its methods. In Bio Art, the methods come from biology and genetics. The bacterial art of Maria Penil Cobo and Mehmet Berkman (see Figure 2.6; see also Chapter 3) and the hybrid cacti of Amy Youngs (see Figure 2.7; see also Chapter 7) fit into this category.

Moving on to the integration of visual art and creative writing, we find many contemporary artists—such as Faith Ringgold, Carmen Lomas Garza, Kerry James Marshall, and Scott Musgrove (see Figure 2.8; see also Chapter 7), as well as graphic novelists or comic book artists such as Nick Sousanis and Chris Ware—adopting the book form and producing narrative art that merges storytelling and visual art.

ART AND INTEGRATED CREATIVE INQUIRY

Why is art practice such a good model for integrated inquiry curriculum? Artists often generate variations on a theme, idea, concept, or feeling that accrue into a body of artwork. Each work an artist creates represents a step in an ongoing exploration of art-based ways to interpret, represent, and convey "findings." Each iteration builds on the artwork and related preparatory work that went before.

Creative art-based inquiry is essentially contemporary art adapted to a learning environment and integrated with pedagogy. It follows the example of contemporary integrative art, in taking the investigative processes of the social and natural sciences and infusing them with the methods and forms of the visual and performing arts, including creative writing.

Creative art-based inquiry resembles scientific inquiry in that it begins with curiosity about a subject, which leads to questions that focus artists' inquiries. From there, artists explore what is known about their topics. This could include the many ways a topic has

been presented or interpreted by other artists or in other disciplines. The next step is generating ideas about what a topic means to an artist or to the world. Graeme Sullivan (2010) calls this an artist's "theory." From there, artists play with ideas and interpretations of their theories. This can involve experiments with materials and images or play with other ways of expressing an artist's perspective on the topic and giving audiences an aesthetic experience with the topic.

Creative inquiry gets much of its energy and distinctiveness through its orientation and employment of methods often associated with particular fields such as

- History and anthropology, because they focus on human cultural experience and employ thick descriptions and stories
- The creative language arts (poetry, descriptive writing, drama, and storytelling), because they have license to imagine and create, to be non-logical and fantastic, and to be subjective and interpretative in their inquiries into reality

KEYS TO UNDERSTANDING

Tenets of Art-Based Curriculum Integration

- Integration is making connections among ideas and topics in the various academic domains. It is seeing how the ideas and topics fit together.
- Integration in art-based inquiry is delving into Big Ideas through creative play, imagination, invention, and transforming/presenting ideas in aesthetic forms and experiences (art).
- Substantive, multidimensional curriculum integration means digging into significant ideas and issues inherent in academic topics and doing it through the many ways professionals in the domains do.
- The visual arts are an excellent vehicle for integration because they have no boundaries, allow for fresh perspectives, and make new and often unconventional connections. Contemporary artworks provide models for integrated thinking and creative connection making.

numberless millennia and struggle against the harshness and brutality of Nature only to die and lie buried beneath Interstate 90 outside of Bend, Oregon? That seems to be the case. In the instance of the Hairy Brook Trout, it doesn't help that he was so delicious.

The scientific community seems to have almost willfully ignored this domestic and, frankly, less-than-glamorous area of study, perhaps afraid of what they'd find, or maybe just kinda grossed out by the sheer fecundity, if not the queer moribundity, of the North American wilderness. Indeed, science had failed to milk this field of study, leaving it unmilked until the Zoological Udder became clogged. Well, I plan to keep tugging and squeezing until the world is verily flooded with the milk of forgotten knowledge! So to speak.

Perils in the field of research: Allergic reaction to partially-untamed llama escort (Louisianna Long-Horned Rental Llama.)

After college, with a few trips to South America under my belt, I began my research in earnest. While all the handsome, credentialed paleontologists with graying manes of hair, pointy English boots and khaki outfits were combing such glamorous locations as the Gobi Desert and the Great Rift Valley looking for high-ticket items like the very macho (and probably imaginary) "Tyrannosaurus Rex," I was clawing my way through the underbrush behind mini malls and under freeway overpasses in search of the forgotten cousins of the Calvus

Mogera Terra (Bald Surface Mole). I unearthed nests of petrified "dog eggs" while being bitten and stung by relatives of the Palorus Subdepressus (Depressed Dinner Beetle) and the Cimex Nigrocinctus! A thankless task? Yes. Oh, hell yes. But one that, soon enough, was to bear unlikely, and revolutionary, fruit.

Let's look at the case of the Dwarf Basket Horse: it was during a routine excavation at the State Penitentiary in West Texas that I first discovered this charming creature. What I initially took to be a peculiar bird skeleton tangled in its own nest turned out to be, in fact, a curious mammal, which would later be known, mostly by me, as the Dwarf Basket Horse.

Early American pioneers encountered these creatures back in the 1800s, describing them in letters sent back East as "horse-seeds"; that is, they apparently thought these were horses growing on trees. Good guess. Unfortunately, the majority of settlers arrived from the South and mistook these things suspended in the trees for piñatas. As a result, the Basket Horses were whacked mercilessly with sticks, the settlers apparently expecting candy.

Due to poor communication, and ignorance of science, word never spread very far that these were not, in fact, piñatas. So, wave after wave of stick-wielding revelers moved across the land, beating the adorable Basket Horse deep into the blood-splattered pages of history. Only a few crude drawings survive to this day. Obviously, these were of little help in my research. However, thanks to my vast knowledge of biology, taxidermy, mammal anatomy, zoology, and…um…horse-ology, I think it's probably called, I was able to reconstruct the

Early Late-Afternoon of the so-called Dwarf Basket Horse.

4

Indeed, the basic strategies of creative writing are the more open and imaginative methods of creative inquiry—and the strategies we find in the arts—while the primary engine of creative inquiry is the human experience and perception (social, cultural, and personal).

Picture your students learning about a topic using the modified scientific process described above infused with the creative methods and lenses of the arts. If this sounds promising, take a look at some examples of integrated inquiry trails described in Chapter 9.

You will most likely find that curriculum integration through art-based creative inquiry is seamless and natural; each topic flows into the next and each connects to the others on multiple levels. That is because of the web of connections among disciplines (the overlaps, intersections, and hybrids) discussed above and the capacity of art and creative inquiry to spin the thread and weave the web. In Part II, I look in some depth at the four disciplines (the areas of inquiry or domains) to provide multiple threads for this web of integration and a strong foundation on which to construct it.

PART II

The Academic Disciplines and Related Art

MEANINGFUL curriculum integration requires a deep, multifaceted understanding of the academic disciplines. This understanding is foundational knowledge on which integrated knowledge is built and from which new knowledge can grow. There are two reasons for this. First, the more we know about something, the more material we have to work with, the richer the exploration, and the deeper the connections. Second, knowing more about the disciplines provides us new, fresh, and interesting ways to integrate them and to teach them.

The chapters in Part II present overviews of the four disciplines whose subjects are taught in schools—the natural sciences (Chapter 3), mathematics (Chapter 4), social studies (Chapter 5), and language arts (Chapter 6). Each chapter goes beyond the subjects investigated to include the ways the disciplines generate knowledge and their purposes for doing so. For this, I look at the disciplines through the lens of Boix-Mansilla and Gardner's (1998) Four Dimensions of Understanding. Introduced in Chapter 2 regarding curriculum integration, these four dimensions cover the basic pillars of the disciplines: the *purpose* of a discipline (why), the *knowledge* a discipline generates (what), the *methods* it uses to generate knowledge (how), and the *forms* it uses to conceptualize and convey knowledge (tools). Using this four-pronged framework helps us to understand the disciplines more comprehensively and, therefore, to design more substantive arts integration.

Note that the subjects taught in schools are different from the professional disciplines (Beane, 2011). School subjects are content areas that often teach the knowledge of the disciplines in isolation. The arts integration proposed in this book aims to go beyond content or knowledge taught in school to bring learners' experiences with school subject areas closer to the practices of adult practitioners in the various domains. That is, the goal is to change the focus of learning away from covering information and toward asking the questions and using the methods and forms disciplinary practitioners use. This has two important implications for learners. First, disciplines are living, evolving areas of curiosity and passionate inquiry. Second, knowledge is not fixed or context free, but instead is something that is ever evolving and responding to its environment.

Although all four disciplines possess the elements of an area of study, each domain calls attention to a specific trait of art and art-based inquiry. The natural sciences provide insight into investigation and the methods and thinking that go into it. Mathematics highlights aesthetic form, order, and abstraction. Social studies is about the subject matter of art. That is because art, no matter the specific topic it addresses, is about human experience, perception, and perspective. While the language arts also stress their roots in human experience and thought, their particular contribution to art-based inquiry is insight into how different modalities work—how they are similar, how they differ, and how they can work together to build on each other to create meaning. Furthermore, storytelling and creative writing highlight the creative strategies in both the visual and the literary arts.

The chapters in Part II are designed to serve as resources for teachers. Each chapter includes examples of research-based contemporary art that addresses concepts in the discipline under discussion.

Chapters 3–6 include information from Marshall and Donahue, *Art-Centered Learning Across the Curriculum* (2014). I cite chapter authors from that book where appropriate.

3

The Natural Sciences
Understanding the Natural World

THE NATURAL SCIENCES can be divided into three primary categories according to the subjects they investigate. These are (1) the *physical sciences,* which study the nature and properties of matter and energy; (2) the *Earth and space sciences,* which focus on the forms and properties of the Earth and the forces that shape it; and (3) the *life sciences,* which study living organisms (Horvath & Marshall, 2014). Each of these general categories includes disciplines that study specific subject areas, such as biology, chemistry, physics, and astronomy, as well as more specialized genres within those areas, such as meteorology, microbiology, and quantum physics. There are also hybrid genres in science, such as ecology and paleontology, that address ideas and subjects from multiple scientific domains and use their various methods to do so.

FOUR DIMENSIONS OF THE NATURAL SCIENCES

How do we get to the essence of the natural sciences? Boix-Mansilla and Gardner's (1998) Four Dimensions of Understanding provide a framework for exploring this question.

Purpose

The natural sciences aim to unlock the secrets of nature; they seek to understand the natural world and to describe and predict natural phenomena (Gauch,

2012). The origins of science are wonder and curiosity. These dispositions drive scientists to

- Investigate and contemplate natural forms and forces—observe closely
- Experiment with possibilities
- Infer probabilities and synthesize what they find
- Connect their findings to other phenomena—generalize
- Peer beneath the surface to discern patterns and laws (Gauch, 2012)

That is to say, scientists look for the underlying order in nature, which is expressed as laws that govern the seemingly chaotic natural world we experience. Two guiding assumptions propel science:

- There is an underlying order in nature.
- The human mind can comprehend that order.

Knowledge

The knowledge of the natural sciences is covered in the Next Generation Science Standards (NGSS) (2013). This knowledge falls into two primary categories.

Information. Information is specific evidence obtained through observation, measurement, and interpretation of phenomena. Because information is gleaned and developed through observations, which can change, it is not permanent, but is open to new interpretations and understandings. The provisional nature of evidence and ideas about it prompts scientists to call their findings and interpretations of them "information" instead of "facts" (Derry, 1999).

Concepts. Concepts constitute the second form of scientific knowledge. Concepts are the connections that tie information together; they are what makes scientific information meaningful (Derry, 1999; Newton, 2012). Scientists discern concepts through analysis, synthesis, and inference. In other words, they take their findings (i.e., their information) and detect their implications—what the findings mean and the concepts they represent. The NGSS (2013) define the core disciplinary concepts in each area of science as follows:

- In the physical sciences: matter, motion, and energy
- In the life sciences: structure and process of organisms and ecosystems, and the mechanisms of heredity and evolution
- In the Earth and space sciences: Earth's placement, Earth-based systems, and the relationship of the Earth and humans

Concepts that span all of the sciences are called *crosscutting concepts*. According to the NGSS (2013), crosscutting concepts in the natural sciences are the following:

- Pattern
- Cause and effect
- Systems and system models
- Scale, proportion, and quantity
- Energy and matter
- Structure and function
- Stability and change

Methods

The natural sciences vary in the kinds of investigations they do. Often the subjects studied determine the kinds of methods used. For example, chemists and physicists can do controlled lab experiments to test

their hypotheses, whereas evolutionary biologists must make inferences from existing evidence. Generally speaking, however, all scientists do the following:

- Ask questions
- Develop and use models
- Plan and carry out investigations
- Analyze and interpret data
- Use mathematics and computational thinking
- Construct explanations
- Develop cases based on evidence
- Obtain, evaluate, and communicate information (Horvath & Marshall, 2014; NGSS, 2013).

Scientists also construct hypotheses and theories, test them, and make predictions (Gauch, 2012; Gimbel, 2011; Newton, 2012). A hypothesis is a scientist's speculation about the meaning or implications of what is found in observations or data. A theory is a hypothesis or an aggregate of hypotheses that holds up to scrutiny (Aicken, 1991; Beveridge, 1950/2004). As an accumulation of evidence built through multiple hypotheses and investigations, a theory has broader range and vision, and a better claim to truth than a hypothesis. A theory, however, is never the whole truth. Instead, it is the current strongest explanation or model of phenomena and, therefore, is open to challenge, modification, and elaboration.

Inquiry Process. Scientists strive to discover something—a new phenomenon, concept, or theory (Derry, 1999)—and they do this in the context of what is already known. Often, scientific findings emerge from the work of many scientists who have either prepared the way for a discovery or work collaboratively to discover something new. That means science is social; scientists work within scientific norms and they build on each other's work (Kuhns, 1962; Latour, 1987).

Scientific inquiry begins with "problem finding," which involves observation of a subject and noticing how knowledge of it is incomplete. Then scientists ask questions about the phenomenon. These are research questions that enable scientists to focus beyond the subject to what they want to know about it.

From there, scientists do background research to see what is already known about a topic. They then

- Locate problems that matter
- Construct experiments
- Think in divergent ways for solving problems
- Recognize patterns and connections
- Discern abstract concepts in specific phenomena
- Project and predict from evidence
- Construct models
- Build an overarching theory

examine (through experimentation or observation) different phenomena or ideas, analyze the results of this examination, make inferences based on results, and test their inferences to construct a theory. For a theory to be viable, it must explain in a logical and economical way why the phenomenon occurs. Not all theories can be completely tested, so scientists go with a theory that best explains phenomena (Kuhns, 1962).

Scientists also construct models—templates for understanding similar or related phenomena based on their theories. Models may be mathematical, graphic, or three-dimensional physical representations. Making models allows scientists to generalize— to apply a theory to other instances and predict what may happen in the future.

Creativity and Scientific Inquiry. A popular misconception about science is that scientific knowledge is based entirely on logic or reason. But frequently scientific inquiry requires and is spurred by intuition and imagination (Aicken, 1991; Ben-Ari, 2005; Bohm, 1998; Derry, 1999; Gauch, 2012; Newton, 2012) or requires nonlogical or associative thinking (Doll, Fleener, Trueit, & St. Julien, 2005). Scientific inquiry entails using imagination to

Imagination is the capacity to see what is not readily apparent (Ricoeur, 1991) or to picture in one's mind how processes work (Beveridge, 1950/2004). Trueit (2005) points out how imagination drives scientific breakthroughs; she describes the imaginative, yet rational logic inherent in scientific inquiry as poietic logic—the fusion of logical and linear thinking with associative and nonlinear thought, as discussed in Chapter 1. This hybrid way of thinking is key to scientific inquiry and also the basis of creative thinking in art and creative inquiry.

According to Brown (2003), the primary creative thinking in science is metaphorical thinking. Metaphor is the casting of one entity as another (Black, 1981; Lakoff & Johnson, 1980; Orotony, 1993). Metaphor may seem rather fanciful, but it is where imagination becomes practical. It is a practical necessity because it bridges what is new and intangible to what we already understand; it allows us to attach abstract ideas and invisible phenomena to something known, tangible, and concrete (Brown, 2003). Scientists rely on metaphor to understand phenomena and also to convey their understandings to others. A metaphor in science can be as simple as picturing neurons as trees and brains as forests (Farinella & Roš, 2013) or as complex and poetic as describing neurons, as Ramón y Cajal did, as the "butterflies of the soul" (DeFelipe, 2010).

Figure 3.1 is an illustration of a nerve cell by Ramón y Cajal, the father of neuroscience, and Figure 3.2 is a drawing by Matteo Farinella depicting Ramón y Cajal standing in a forest of neurons sketching them. Farinella is also a neuroscientist and a comic book artist who writes and illustrates books about the brain and the nervous system. His metaphorical illustrations of nerves and the nervous system provide a basis for Farinella's storytelling about neuroscientists and their work.

FIGURE 3.1. Santiago Ramón y Cajal, *Purkinje Cell* (1899)

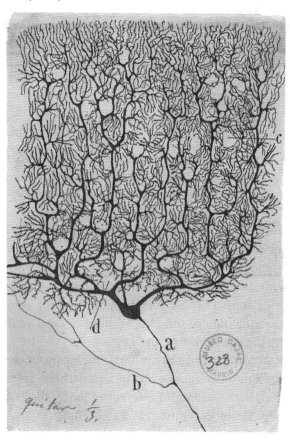

FIGURE 3.2. Matteo Farinella, Page from *Neurocomic* (Farinella & Roš, 2013, p. 16)

Forms

The forms of a discipline are the tools practitioners use to conceptualize and convey their findings and ideas. It is impressive how many forms of science are visual. They include illustrations, maps, charts, diagrams, and models. A majority of these visual forms are unambiguous, unadorned, and purely informational. However, many scientific visuals, such as botanical illustrations, cosmological maps, and geological survey maps, mix information and metaphor, and they are beautiful.

COMPARING SCIENCE AND ART

To draw comparisons between science and art, I turn again to Boix-Mansilla and Gardner's (1998) Four Dimensions of Understanding.

Purpose

How do science and art compare in purpose? Both observe and interpret nature in an effort to understand and appreciate it. Indeed, art and science come from a common origin: wonder and curiosity (Bohm, 1998; Strauss, 2013). Scientists, such as David Bohm (1998) and educator Mary Jo Pollman (2017), claim that artists and scientists are also motivated by the beauty they observe in nature. Ironically, it seems scientists today are more preoccupied with the beauty of nature and natural forms than contemporary artists are (Ede, 2005). Many contemporary artists focus on other things—addressing big nature-related questions such as these:

- Where do we fit into nature?
- How does nature affect us?
- How does nature provide models for architecture and design?

- What can we learn from nature?
- How can we care for nature?

Going further, contemporary artists look beyond nature to address how science understands nature and, more important, how the scientific perspective influences the way we think about and act toward the natural world. That is to say, art encourages us to look critically at science and its cultural consequences. Art has, in many cases, moved beyond the primarily aesthetic, illustration, and chronicling purposes it held prior to postmodernism and toward cultural critique. Going forward, artists have taken on the role of deep thinkers about big issues related to nature, the environment, and science. They also have taken on the mantle of creative problem solvers to help scientists and decision makers find solutions to environmental problems (Ede, 2005).

Knowledge

Regarding knowledge, this is where art and science differ the most. Science discovers and constructs new information and pursues understandings aimed to be enduring, concrete, and grounded in evidence (Aicken, 1991; Ben-Ari, 2005; Derry, 1999). For its part, art does not create information or "facts" but brings new perspectives to information (Sullivan, 2010). That is, the knowledge of art is the insights and perspectives of artists. Art is personal, but it also can reflect or enrich the understandings and experiences of nature and science for the artist and for viewers. Generally speaking, science generates the knowledge, and art makes it meaningful (Ede, 2005). Here we find the primary reason for employing art when we teach science: Art can make academic study of science more meaningful. However, art can also generate knowledge. One example is the Crochet Coral Reef Project (refer to Figure 4.2), in which artists invent new hyperbolic forms with each new iteration of the project, and new insights into the emergent nature of the creative process have developed (Wertheim, 2015).

Methods

Art and science also share inquiry methods and ways of thinking. This was touched on earlier in the discussion of poietic logic and scientific inquiry. Both science and art entail observation, experimentation, analysis, and logical reasoning; both involve imagination and creative thinking; and both engage in constructive play. In science and art, creative thinking is necessary for finding problems and solving them. Addressing problems is only one part of both domains, however. They also entail vision and imagination that go beyond creative approaches to problems. But the two diverge in how rule-bound they are. While the sciences require objectivity and replicable outcomes, art does not. Art is subjective and personal; it can fly into fantasy and nonsense, and it shuns replication.

Forms

Regarding forms, scientists and artists both use visual images to record what they see (what is visible) and to visualize what they think, imagine, or know from reasoning (what is invisible). Most important, artists and scientists *develop* ideas, concepts, and understandings by making visual imagery (Samuel, 2014; Strauss, 2013). Indeed, making visible the concepts that lie behind sense perception is how both science and art come to understand the natural world.

Traditionally, artists have communicated their ideas, understandings, and emotions through the forms of art, such as portraits, still lifes, landscapes, and abstract designs, while scientists have conveyed their findings and thinking in the visual formats associated with science: maps, diagrams, illustrations, and observational drawings. Today, many artists dispense with the traditional visual formats of art and instead use science-based visual forms to convey their ideas. In bringing the "visual vocabulary" of science into art, these artists convey ideas in ways we recognize from science and bring fresh modes of expression to art.

EXAMPLES OF ART THAT EXPLORES CROSSCUTTING CONCEPTS

Nature has forever been a subject and an inspiration for artists. A source of metaphors, symbols, and decorative patterns, nature has also provided ideas for architecture and design. The depiction of natural forms in still lifes, landscapes, and natural history

KEYS TO UNDERSTANDING

Comparing Art and the Natural Sciences

Comparing science with art provides the opportunity to explore investigative processes and the creativity inherent in both domains.

- Both are areas of inquiry with their origins in wonder and curiosity.
- Both have similar processes of investigation and exploration of the natural world that include asking questions, observing, experimenting, making inferences, constructing models, and devising interpretations.
- Both use metaphor to understand and communicate phenomena or ideas.
- Both use visual forms and images to record what is seen, to develop ideas, and to convey ideas (images of perception and images of conception).

Scientists and Artists

- Are curious and wonder about the world and our place in it.
- Ask questions; challenge foregone conclusions and habits of mind.
- Build upon existing structures and knowledge to go into the unknown.
- Engage in creative thinking, strategies, and process in both investigation and interpretation.
- Mix logical and linear thinking with imaginative, nonlinear thinking.
- Apply ideas, structures, and methods of one discipline to another. These include metaphor, modeling, and mapping.
- Make use of chance intuition, mistakes, and the "prepared mind."
- Improvise and think flexibly.
- Persevere with commitment.
- Find joy and satisfaction in learning and discovery.

illustrations is probably the best-known application of art to nature. Contemporary artists have added another dimension to the exploration of nature. They make art about the concepts embodied in natural forms and forces—the concepts delineated in the Next Generation Science Standards (NGSS, 2013). Here are some examples.

Systems, Cause-and-Effect

Bernie Lubell makes the most whimsical of contraptions. These machines hint at having a purpose, but mostly they move and make noises. Lubell's gadgets are the work of a tinkerer and mad inventor. They remind us of Rube Goldberg's cartoons of whimsical contrivances that perform simple tasks in very convoluted and playful ways. Although the effects may be negligible, the causal trail is complex and surprising. Like Goldberg's machines, Lubell's work makes basic physics fun. Each installation engages the viewer in "running" them or putting them in motion. The work shown in Figure 3.3, *Up in the Air/Le Canard* (2015), is a mechanical system reminiscent of a biological one. As the wooden pulleys turn, the blimp-shaped balloon inflates. Constructed as part of a series on airships, this "ship" is part of Lubell's inquiry into air and breath. In one work, Lubell plays with two concepts in science and nature: systems and cause-and-effect.

Systems

Maria Penil Cobo works with scientist Mehmet Berkman to create bacterial art (refer to Figure 2.6). Interested in small ecosystems, Penil cultivates colorful bacteria, paints them in petri dishes, and lets them grow. In doing so, she makes the invisible world visible. Her goal is to reveal the beauty of the microscopic world to change public opinion of bacteria from fear and disgust to appreciation and curiosity. In this work, the artist employs the natural processes of bacteria to portray a system: the brain. Penil Cobo is one of many artists working with scientists (such as Berkman) in the genre of Bio Art.

Structure and Function

Brian Jungen creates forms that mimic the structures of animals. In his *Carapace* (2009) (see Figure 3.4), Jungen fabricated a shell-like structure out of plastic tubs to make a refuge from the modern world. In *Cetology* (2002) (see Figure 3.5), he created a whale skeleton out of plastic chairs. These two artworks are examples of how phenomena studied in one discipline (zoology) connect to concepts associated with other domains—how rich, varied, and transdisciplinary art can be. For example, *Carapace* alludes to Native American architecture and its origins in natural structures, while *Cetology* evokes spirituality and the sublime. *Cetology,* in particular, harks back to the wonder and awe we feel when we encounter nature. Reminiscent of displays in natural history museums, this ethereal work reminds us that science and spirituality come from a common source.

Have you ever wanted to sit on a cloud? Michael Arcega invites you to lounge on one in his whimsical cloud-shaped benches in San Francisco's Chinatown (see Figure 3.6). Inspired by clouds in Asian (Taoist and Buddhist) art, these pieces of public art present a puzzle: Strong, material, and firmly planted on the ground, these benches float like fluffy, amorphous shapes in the sky. Clouds may be elusive and ephemeral, but they are also enduring cultural symbols. Here we see how design can stretch the boundaries of structure, and natural forms can be the inspiration for cultural and spiritual symbols.

Energy and Matter

One of the best places to see and experience art about natural forces and forms is the Exploratorium in San Francisco, California. The Exploratorium is a science museum where displays not only demonstrate physical phenomena but are also art.

FIGURE 3.3. Bernie Lubell, *Up in the Air/Le Canard* (2015)

FIGURE 3.4. Brian Jungen, *Carapace* (2009)

FIGURE 3.5. Brian Jungen, *Cetology* (2002)

FIGURE 3.6. Michael Arcega, *Auspicious Clouds | Heavy Fog* (2018). Ramona Arcega is sitting on the piece.

FIGURE 3.7. Shawn Lani, *Geyser* (2013)

Most of the Exploratorium's displays are created by resident artists/designers to be beautiful, imaginative, and engaging artwork that is also informative. These works are particularly impressive in the way they recreate natural forces and systems, which move and generate patterns and forms according to forces such as temperature, air and water pressure, magnetism, gravity, and inertia.

Shawn Lani, a senior artist and curator at the Exploratorium, designs displays that merge art with education. One example is *Geyser* (2013), in the Exploratorium's Gallery of Living Systems (see Figure 3.7). Lani's geyser erupts periodically according to changing water temperature and pressure. In this artwork, we see how matter and energy collide and how beautiful it can be when that happens.

Patterns

While pattern is a crosscutting concept in nature, it is also a key formal element in visual art—from folk art, to the decorative arts, to more conceptual and contemporary art. If you look closely at the artworks in this book, you will see that many of them have patterns. Fred Tomaselli is an artist who is obsessed with patterns. In his *Big Bird* (2004), Tomaselli contrasts the patterning on the bird with the patterns of the leaves and stars that surround it (see Figure 3.8). Here Tomaselli alludes to the underlying patterns in all of nature. This concept is also addressed in Tony Cragg's *Spyrogyra*, which directly illustrates the spiral pattern of growth and structure in plant life (see Figure 3.9).

EXAMPLES OF ART INSPIRED BY SCIENCE

Contemporary artists also go beyond a focus on nature to concentrate on the workings of science. They do this in three distinct ways. First, some artists use the formats and memes of the natural sciences to convey ideas. Jason Freeny, for example, plays with the formats and memes of scientific illustration in his humorous sculptures and images that conflate artificial animals (cultural icons and toys) with the real animals upon which they are based (see Figure 3.10).

FIGURE 3.8. Fred Tomaselli, *Big Bird* (2004)

FIGURE 3.9. Tony Cragg, *Spyrogyra* (1992)
Sir Tony Cragg (England, b. 1949)
Spyrogyra 1992 glass and steel, 220 × 210 cm
Art Gallery of New South Wales
Mervyn Horton Bequest Fund 1997 © Anthony Cragg
Photo: Diana Panuccio, AGNEW 292.1997

Hine Mizushima uses a similar strategy and also references a source of her scientific formats and visual vocabulary: natural history museums. Her "museum specimens" are invented hybrid animals and enlarged microscopic animals—creatures we could never see with the naked eye because they are either imaginary or too tiny to observe with a simple magnifying glass (refer to Figures 2.4 and 2.5).

Second, artists use the tools and methods of scientists in their art making. For example, Maria Penil Cobo uses the tools, methods, and materials of science in her bacterial art (refer to Figure 2.6).

Third, artists explore the implications of scientific knowledge. This often translates into illustrated science fiction. Scott Musgrove's book *The Late Fauna of Early North America* (2009) is a work of visual art science fiction. In it, Musgrove imagines and illustrates imaginary animals of the past, much like natural historians and paleontologists do (refer to Figure 2.8; see also Chapter 7).

KEYS TO UNDERSTANDING

Creative Inquiry into the Natural Sciences

- Address the core concepts of the natural sciences through creative inquiry. Connect the Big Ideas (abstractions) to the specific (concrete).
- Use the methods and forms of the sciences as strategies to explore the concepts (research methods and presentation methods such as diagramming, mapping, and charting).
- Look at the disciplines of the physical sciences, Earth and space sciences, and life sciences as active areas of inquiry that continue to construct and revise knowledge. See and explore the content of the disciplines in the ways practicing researchers in the disciplines do.

FIGURE 3.10. Jason Freeny, *Cootie* (ND)

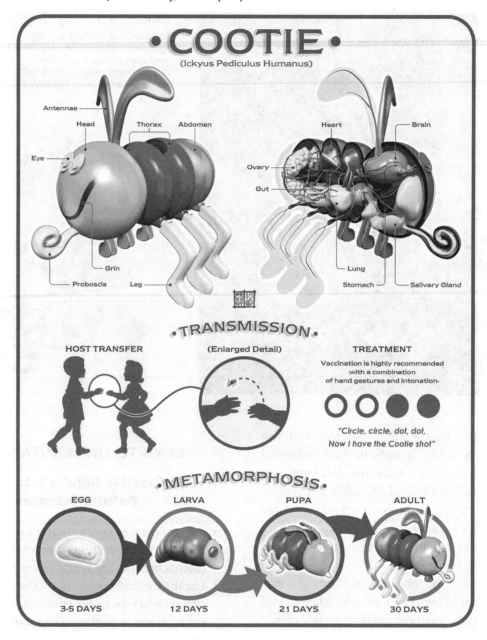

INTEGRATING SCIENCE AND ART IN THE CLASSROOM

When we integrate art and science, we explore three different subjects: nature, science, and art. That is, nature is studied through the lens of both science and art to reveal patterns, forces, and forms of natural phenomena, including systems both in living organisms and in the inorganic phenomena that shape the physical world.

To investigate natural forms and forces, learners can use the tools and methods of the natural sciences—such as microscopes, telescopes, stethoscopes, thermometers, spring scales, collection nets, measuring cups, graduated cylinders, and anemometers—to explore matter and then make art about what they find. Furthermore, they might grow plants from seeds and dissect them to see their parts; or they can examine hair, skin cells, and insect wings under a microscope; they can measure and record the gait of their dog or record the number of hours their cat sleeps each day. Also, observations and experiments can be augmented with visits to natural history museums. A hands-on science museum, such as the Exploratorium in San Francisco, is a great place to play with and study natural forces.

All of these studies and field trips can be interpreted and recorded in learners' research workbooks (see Chapter 7). Throughout the investigative process, learners are encouraged to make art that interprets and further explores their findings and insights from their scientific observations and experiments. Any and all of this can be the subject of art, but to truly have meaning, the images must be more than simple illustrations; they should reveal a learner's thinking about a phenomenon or connect the specific subject to related concepts in science and nature. That is, illustrations should bear personal interpretation and have conceptual content. An example of one way to do this is demonstrated in the first curriculum trail described in Chapter 9 (see Figure 9.1).

The study of nature through mimicking scientists prepares learners for examining science itself, including what scientists do. Furthermore, learners' attention can be directed toward the inquiry process and creativity inherent in both science and art, and comparing the two domains. How does a teacher go about this? One way is to have learners read stories about scientists' and artists' visions and lives, and how they work. Another is for learners to record and map what they are doing in their investigations and compare it to what they read about scientists and artists.

Questions about process help learners focus on inquiry in science, art, and learning. To facilitate this, a teacher can ask learners guiding questions about what they are doing each step of the way and use the action words of inquiry common to both science and art, such as: investigate, observe, explore, experiment, measure, guess, discover, connect, interpret, problem-solve, make, and imagine. When learners observe what they do, even in the most rudimentary way, they build a deeper understanding of what it means to be an inquirer—in both art and science.

The examples of art related to science and nature presented in this chapter are just the tip of the iceberg. There are so many ways artists address nature and science and interact with scientists. It follows, then, that there are many models for learners to study nature and science through art—from printing plant forms; to mapping the life cycle of a butterfly; to picturing theories about molecules, weather patterns, global climate change, and the stars; to growing ecosystems in petri dishes.

Furthermore, there are multiple ways for art and science to integrate in creative inquiry. One way is to enliven and extend the study of nature in the science curriculum by applying the creative strategies of art and learning presented in Chapter 7. Metaphor, in particular, can help learners understand phenomena because it connects what they are learning about to what they already know (Wormeli, 2009).

- How are rivers the veins of a landscape?
- How is a human cell equivalent to a school or a family?
- How are beehives cities, and we the bees?
- How are the layers of Earth a ladder back in time?

Metaphor and metaphorical questions like these also impel learners to comprehend topics more deeply and imaginatively. This is why metaphor is such an effective strategy for teaching (Wormeli, 2009) and why scientists are so engaged with metaphors (Brown, 2003).

The bottom line is that the strategies and practices of making art and visual imagery—playing with ideas, and projecting further or following the "what if?"—bring active, tactile, experiential, aesthetic, and imaginative play to the study of science and nature. And because art and scientific inquiry have so much in common, art can make the study of science more like what creative scientists actually *do* than what common content-based academic study can do.

4

Mathematics

Logic and Abstraction Meet Application and Aesthetics

MATH is the language of numbers, patterns, and relationships (Devlin, 1994). We use math every day when we calculate quantities, estimate distances, and keep track of time. Math is so much a part of life and so essential to navigating our world that it is easy to forget what a marvel it is. Most of us tend to *use* math rather than understand it or appreciate it beyond its most practical and commonplace functions. The objective of this chapter is to go beyond calculation to get at the substance and meaning of mathematics, as well as to demonstrate its relationship to art. I want to encourage teachers to go beyond simply using math as a practical tool to make art (measuring, calculating, and using geometric shapes) to making art to explore mathematical concepts.

FOUR DIMENSIONS OF MATHEMATICS

As with other academic disciplines, developing an understanding of math calls for examining its four dimensions (Boix-Mansilla & Gardner, 1998).

Purpose

The earliest purpose of mathematics was to give numerical representation or value to quantities of things in the world. It allowed people to quantify and to work flexibly with those quantities, and to count, add, subtract, multiply, and divide quantities represented by numbers (Cossey & Donahue, 2014). These calculation processes are as old as ancient Egypt and Babylonia and represent practical applications to real-world problems.

Algebra, the form that developed after simple arithmetic, is the study of operations and relationships that enables us to access unknown quantities. An algebraic equation sets up a relationship between known quantities and equivalent unknown quantities. The equation, therefore, is a puzzle in which a piece is missing; when we know the value of one quantity, we can figure out the value of the missing piece. About 500 BCE, geometry—the study of shape, size, space, and the relative position of objects—extended the realm of math. The purpose of geometry is to map out space in numerical relationships and to enable the computation of relationships in space. For instance, the Pythagorean Theorem provides us with a formula for calculating the length of the sides of a right-angle triangle (Cossey & Donahue, 2014). The Pythagorean Theorem exemplifies Euclidean geometry.

Math finds many of its purposes and usefulness in the sciences. When scientists describe natural forces and forms, they use numbers and numerical relationships, and they make mathematical models that they can apply elsewhere. Also, numerical calculations and projections can prove scientific hypotheses and theories. In a nutshell, math—with its numbers, formulas, equations, and geometry—enables scientists to

- Discern and describe patterns, structures, and relationships in the world

- Make precise calculations
- Convey findings and mathematical ideas succinctly and concretely
- Make predictions

Math is about connecting the dots (the ancient Greeks literally did that to create geometric shapes [Devlin, 2000]). Math is also about finding abstract forms (such as circles or spheres) in oranges and planets, about cycles and rotations in movement, and about distilling down complex systems into a universal language. Therefore, math is about moving from the concrete to the abstract, often going from concrete problems and observations (adding three toes to four fingers to calculate seven "digits") and moving to abstraction (seeing how numbers stand alone as quantities). For example, three apples represent the same amount as three oranges or three fingers, and this understanding allows a number to become an independent concept that can be applied elsewhere. Mathematics also is concrete; it allows us to express abstractions and abstract patterns in the concrete and specific language of numbers.

Math may have its origins in everyday life; it also can stand on its own, separate from mundane uses. In the complex and "pure" math of today, formulas, procedures, and theorems are far more abstract and detached from our sense-based practical world. Math problems are often puzzles constructed from a universe of mathematical knowledge that challenges the logic and imagination of mathematicians. That is not to say that all those arcane math problems in today's theoretical and pure math are devoid of purpose. Game theory, for example, is a field that draws on abstract mathematical models to describe and predict how humans, rational or not, interact with each other. This theory applies to any "play," including games, markets, and international diplomacy.

Knowledge

Each area of math, whether it is basic algebra, geometry, calculus, or game theory, has its own area of knowledge. Math has, however, key knowledge—ideas and concepts—common to all branches of the domain. These concepts are pattern, abstraction, and aesthetics.

Pattern. Mathematician Kevin Devlin (1994) describes math as the study of patterns. Devlin cites "numerical patterns, patterns of shape, patterns of motion, patterns of behavior" (p. 3), and the patterns we construct in our minds. Undoubtedly, these patterns are more than visual patterns but are primarily conceptual patterns—patterns of order, structure, and logical relationships. Looking at the world through the lens of patterns enables us to see the underlying order in what may seem to be chaos. Translating these patterns into mathematical formulas reveals the implicit structure of nature. Once we see that structure, our vision of the world becomes more holistic. Prime examples of this systemic, mathematical vision are seeing fractal geometry in trees, clouds, and coastlines; noticing the Fibonacci sequence in succulents and celery stalks; and observing non-Euclidean geometry in lettuce and corals.

Abstraction. Abstraction is the distillation of complex phenomena into concepts. In math, abstraction includes quantifying—expressing amounts in numbers. Quantifying allows us to describe patterns and understand complex phenomena in clear and precise ways. In math, abstraction extends to general rules and principles, such as "the rule of sum," which pertains to addition, and "the rule of product," which pertains to multiplication. Rules like these come from specific mathematical problems and are applied to solve other problems (Cossey & Donahue, 2014). That is to say, they are abstractions we can apply to concrete instances. Abstractions are also simplifications of complex forms. For example, daisies and other flowers are primarily circular, while bubbles and planets are spherical. Life cycles and other repetitive processes are also understood as circles.

Aesthetics. Of the four school disciplines (natural science, math, social studies, and language arts), math is the one most associated with aesthetics. That is because math is the language of proportion, balance, scale, symmetry, and harmony—attributes associated with beauty in the visual world. Mathematicians strive to create beautiful theorems, formulas, and solutions. They also create visual forms that not only convey information but are beautiful (Lima, 2014, 2017). In math, beauty implies elegance, simplicity, and clarity

KEYS TO UNDERSTANDING

Kinds of Geometry and Geometric Patterns

- **Fibonacci Sequence.** A simple, regular pattern in which the next number is the sum of the two numbers before it: 1 + 1 = 2; 1 + 2 = 3; 2 + 3 = 5; 3 + 5 = 8; 5 + 8 = 13; 8 + 13 = 21; and so forth (Devlin, 1994). This numerical pattern is found in plants, sea shells, bone structures (the proportion of bones in hands), and the reproduction rate of rabbits. It is the basis for the Golden Mean (Devlin, 1994).
- **Euclidean Geometry.** The geometry of flat surfaces and solid objects first systematized by Euclid (3rd century BCE). This simple geometry of flat surfaces has been the basis for geometry since, and is still taught in schools today (Devlin, 1994).
- **Non-Euclidean Geometry**
  - *Spherical Geometry* is the geometry of convex surfaces of spheres like planets and, therefore, it is the geometry of cartographers. Spherical geometry challenges one of Euclidean geometry's primary tenets: parallel lines remain parallel; they never cross (Wertheim, 2015).
  - *Hyperbolic Geometry* is the geometry of convex curves. Hyperbolic geometry challenges a primary tenet of Euclidean geometry: parallel lines remain parallel and never diverge. In hyperbolic geometry, parallel lines diverge to create curvilinear surfaces that are both convex and concave. This allows these forms to have maximum surface areas. Hyperbolic curves and geometry are found in lettuce, seaweed, and corals (Wertheim, 2015).
  - *Fractal Geometry* describes natural complex and irregular forms and movement. Fractals are repeating, self-similar mathematical patterns (repeating similar shapes at different scales). As with the other non-Euclidean geometries, fractal geometry enables us to map the complexity of nature. Through fractals we "mathematize" the patterns behind the turbulence of waves, the shapes of clouds and galaxies, and the self-similar structures of brains, neurons, and cauliflower (Mandelbrot, 1983).

of formulas and theorems that distill and abstract. Beauty lies in clear, elegant statements of "truth" (Devlin, 2000). Math's role in aesthetics is further discussed later in this chapter.

Methods

Mathematical methods are more than simple operations such as addition and multiplication. Each area of math has its own way of operating. What unites these methods is the way mathematicians think, particularly how they think flexibly and use logic, imagination, or intuition (Cossey & Donahue, 2014).

Thinking Logically. Logic is the core of math. Mathematicians often follow their intuition to consider a particular problem but, ultimately, it is logic that shapes and propels mathematical process. Logic allows mathematicians to realize patterns in the world, develop models based on those patterns, and claim their models are "true" (Cossey & Donahue, 2014).

Thinking Imaginatively. While the lockstep of logic is at the core of math, mathematicians push beyond it; they extend math beyond what they consider true. Here they use imagination. Imagination is seeing something that is not already there (Ricoeur, 1991). Imagination comes into play when mathematicians approach new problems, unsolved math puzzles, or limits to thinking in accounting for phenomena that cannot be explained by current theories. As in all disciplines, even math, discovery, problem finding, and problem solving require imagination.

Thinking Flexibly. Mathematicians are flexible in their thinking and application of their ideas. They can also be quite amenable to breaking rules, especially since problems in the real world are not always exact and require only moderately accurate or precise conclusions.

Forms

Math is a language with numbers as its basic symbols. Numbers, as symbols, represent the abstract idea of quantity and are used in symbolic forms of math: equations, formulas, and theorems. Geometric shapes

KEYS TO UNDERSTANDING

Some Questions in Mathematics

- How do numbers represent quantities? How do we use math every day to know about quantities of things, and to add, subtract, multiply, and divide them?
- Why is mathematics the "language of nature"? What numbers, patterns, mathematical sequences, and geometric relationships do we see in nature? How does close observation of natural forms and forces reveal the complex geometry inherent in them?
- How does a mathematical model or a set of mathematical rules (algorithms) enable us to understand and predict complex, seemingly chaotic behavior and phenomena?
- How do statistics (numbers) reveal information and make it clear, concrete, and usable?
- How is math grounded in lived experience and observation? How is it a construct of logic and imagination?
- Why do we "boil" things down to numbers, numerical relationships, and geometric forms?
- What forms and mathematical relationships (proportions) are considered beautiful and why?

are also mathematical forms. They represent the spaces between points and lines. As in all disciplines, the forms of math are tools that enable mathematicians to conceptualize ideas and solve problems.

INTERSECTION OF MATH AND ART

The relationship of math to art is ancient and widespread, with each culture having its own sense of aesthetics based on compositional formulas and patterning. Take, for example, the artistic and architectural traditions of China, Japan, Korea, and India, where balance, shape, form, scale, and patterning endow Hindu, Buddhist, and Taoist temples with beauty and spiritual meaning. Another example is the mosques of the Muslim world, which are constructed according to mathematical formulas and covered with tiles arranged in geometric designs or tessellations.

In Euro-American cultures, the notion that ideal visual form and composition can be distilled down into mathematical formulas has a long history, beginning with the classical art and architecture of ancient Egypt and Greece. It continued with Gothic cathedrals of medieval Europe, which were built on their own aesthetic rubrics of shape, pattern, and scale. In ancient Egypt and Greece and in medieval Europe, aesthetic relationships also created stable structures and had symbolic meaning (stability, power, and eternity in Egypt; rationality and ideal form for Greece; and faith, power, and transcendence in medieval Europe).

In the European Renaissance, the classical aesthetics of Greece and Egypt, particularly the Golden Mean, reappeared. The Renaissance was the new age of the Golden Mean and its reign over aesthetic taste and composition. Based on the Fibonacci sequence, the Golden Mean is the geometric formula of growth patterns and proportions in nature. With the Golden Mean, balance, harmony, and proportion are systemized into geometric formulas and applied to art. The rule of the Golden Mean was so solidified in the Renaissance that its formulas are still taught in art classes today.

Geometry and math have always been, by necessity, driving forces in architecture. They became the driving force in 20th-century European art with the "principles of design" (balance, contrast, emphasis, movement, pattern, rhythm, unity, and variety) articulated by the Bauhaus. The "mathematical turn" also arrived at the same time in the austere formalism of the geometric paintings of Piet Mondrian and culminated in the 1970s with the stark geometrical and math-based artwork of artists such as Sol LeWitt.

Abstraction of this sort continues today in the world of design and architecture, but the allure of pure, simple form on its own, for its own sake, has waned in postmodern architecture and contemporary visual art. Artists and architects still play with geometry, though not the simple Euclidean geometry of the ancient Greeks or the Renaissance but, rather, non-Euclidean geometry (refer to Figure 3.7, by Shawn Lani, *Geyser* [2013], as well as works by Margaret and Christine Wertheim and Erik and Martin Demaine discussed later in this chapter). These artworks, along with art that uses algorithms to make patterns (see

Figure 4.1, by Timea Tihanyi, *Burst and Follow, Control and Release. Viral Version Rule #5* [2018]), exemplify how art keeps up with advances in math.

Today, the haven of simpler math is in the contemporary crafts, particularly in quilts, basket weaving, knitting, and crochet work. In these artforms, art and math unite in often repetitive and rhythmic processes and simple geometric forms and patterns to create works that are soothing, contemplative, and often associated with the spiritual.

EXAMPLES OF ART INSPIRED BY CONCEPTS IN MATH

Here I describe three ways in which art can illustrate conceptual patterns, abstraction, and quantities, and how artists explore or use mathematical principles in their art-making process. We see in these works the intersection of pattern, abstraction, and aesthetics.

Patterns and Algorithms

Timea Tihanyi uses current technology to create artworks out of natural materials such as glass and clay. The cylinders in Figure 4.1 are porcelain (ceramic) vessels constructed by 3D printing. To add to the incongruity of materials and process, each vessel is covered with algorithm-generated patterns based on a mathematical model of cellular automata. A cellular automaton is a grid of "cells" in which each cell changes over time according to a defined set of rules that includes the states of neighboring cells. There are many different rules governing automata. Cellular automata have been used for computer modeling of complex systems in nature, and their growth, sustainability, and reproduction.

FIGURE 4.1. Timea Tihanyi, *Burst and Follow, Control and Release. Viral Version Rule #5* (2018)

Each one of Tihanyi's vessels is a unique variation based on the rules applied to the growth of a pattern. Each embodies the surprising mix of high-tech methods, complex mathematical modeling, and traditional craft materials. Crafts are usually considered hands-on and handmade. Part of their allure is the variability, earthiness, and irregularity in patterning. Here Tihanyi breaks all those rules.

Hyperbolic Forms and Non-Euclidean Geometry

The Crochet Coral Reef project (see Figure 4.2) is a multipart collaboration of artists from around the world who have come together in groups under the guidance of Margaret and Christine Wertheim to crochet coral-like forms. These crochet coral reefs are composed of fanciful, colorful hyperbolic forms that mimic real corals and can only be constructed through the looping of threads in crochet. This project is a clear example of contemporary art exploring non-Euclidean geometry and the algorithms behind it. It is also a model of creative art-based inquiry because it is grounded in scientific research into corals and hyperbolic form and has pushed that inquiry further through the process of making art. That is, these artists apply and play with the mathematical rules of hyperbolic form, but also have the freedom to deviate from those codes to invent new forms. Out of this comes an understanding of both art and nature: Art evolves organically over time through improvising on established concepts and conventions in much the same way as life forms evolve through small mutations of existing forms. As the Wertheim sisters suggest, an insight such as this could only emerge from a hands-on creative process.

Math, Form, and Meaning

Martin and Erik Demaine make complex and lyrical paper artworks out of what they call "self-folding origami." When paper is folded along curved creases, it automatically shapes itself into rounded forms that have natural equilibrium. The Demaines are particularly interested in the mysteries of curved creases and surfaces. They are also interested in how various swirling parts (equilibria) can come together to create

more complex structures that mimic chaotic forms and forces in nature (dissipative structures like whirlpools, waves, and galaxies) and allude to non-Euclidean geometry. The artwork in Figure 4.3 illustrates one principle of chaos—the cycle of destruction and creation. Beautiful hyperbolic forms emerge out of the cuts and folds that obscure the text of Graham Greene's story *The Destructors*. The gist of the text is lost through the process of creating a new order.

INTEGRATING MATH AND ART IN THE CLASSROOM

Mathematics is most often taught in K–5 classrooms as a series of disconnected facts and formulas to be memorized or as discrete skills to be mastered. But mathematics is far more than that. It is a system based

---

KEYS TO UNDERSTANDING

Creative Art-Based Inquiry into Mathematics

- Address the core concepts of math by researching the concepts and their manifestations in the natural world, in architecture and design, and in observational drawings and sculpture.
- Play with form and patterns. Construct images and objects based on patterns and design principles from mathematics.
- Gather and quantify information about a topic of interest to students and use graphic methods and symbols of math, such as diagramming, mapping, and charting, in art that addresses those topics.
- Look at the disciplines of mathematics as active areas of inquiry that continue to construct and revise knowledge, particularly in areas (such as game theory) that describe and explain complex phenomena.
- Study mathematicians and how they came to their ideas and discoveries. Explore the personalities and stories behind mathematics and make metaphorical portraits of them.
- Study the history of math, and the cultural and historical factors that shaped mathematical thinking and invention.

FIGURE 4.2. Margaret Wertheim and Christine Wertheim and the Institute for Figuring, *Irish Satellite Reef* from the Crochet Coral Reef project

FIGURE 4.3. Erik Demaine and Martin Demaine, *Destructor IV*, from the *Destructor* Series (2013–2015)

on concrete problems and rooted in the personal observation, imagination, and logic of mathematicians. Knowing about the core ideas of math and understanding the human side of mathematical inventions prepares children for a deeper appreciation of mathematics that will serve them well as they progress in their learning of math. In the following sections I discuss art-based ways to explore a mathematical concept, to recognize math forms in our bodies, and to illustrate the human beings behind mathematical discoveries and thinking.

Abstraction and Instances

Pollman (2017) maintains that learning to think abstractly is a difficult challenge for young children. This begs the question *How can we approach math with children in a way that helps them make the leap from concrete to abstract and back again?* One way is to concept map a number. Concept mapping connects abstract concepts, in this case numbers, to concrete entities (see Chapter 7 for an in-depth discussion of concept mapping). Figure 4.4 is an example of a map that explores the concept of two.

Beginning with the concept map, learners can investigate the meaning of two. They can then make visual images of entities that come in pairs. These pairs often fall into two categories: partners (similar things) or opposites (completely different things). Learners can record all the pairs they find in their bodies, classroom, homes, and neighborhoods. They might identify all the things they find that are two inches long or whose lengths can be evenly divided by two. They can explore how two underlies bilateral symmetry by looking at natural forms such as slices of apples or any vegetable or fruit cut vertically. They might explore how opposites come in twos. Two is particularly easy to work with, but other small numbers work as well. Think about the possibilities of three, four, and five.

Concept maps of numbers are best done in groups. They benefit from group thinking, but once they are created, learners can branch off and explore one of the "instances" of a number on their own. They can integrate math with science by drawing and arranging all their "instances" in a "taxonomy," much like a naturalist would do. Or they can look for twos in natural forms or consider how cause-and-effect can be boiled down to "step one" and "step two." How about imagination? One way to bring in imagination is to ask the questions, What would it be like if everything came in pairs? What would it be like if I (a one) had a double (another me, a two)?

FIGURE 4.4. Map of the Concept of Two

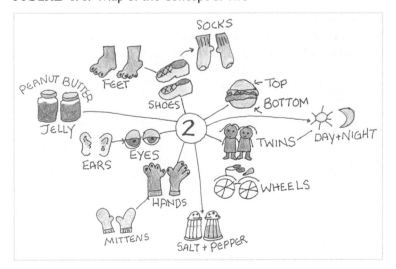

Math and Forms in Nature

Galileo famously said that mathematics is the language of nature. That means numbers, shapes, and mathematical relationships can be found in natural forms. There are many ways to go about this. One way is to explore the math in our bodies—notice the bilateral symmetry in our facial features, arms, and legs; and notice the regular and countable rhythm of our pulse. Creating artwork that conveys these concepts could involve illustrating the symmetry in human bodies (think da Vinci's Vitruvian Man), or inking paper and folding it to create symmetrical forms and patterns, or making tessellations (regular patterns of geometric shapes with no gaps or overlaps). We can also integrate art and math in more meaningful ways, such as exploring the patterns and proportions in pinecones, sunflowers, roses, and celery clusters described by the Fibonacci sequence (see Chapter 9).

Mathematicians and Mathematical Thinking

Thinking mathematically is a human enterprise. People not only see math in things around them and use math to solve problems, they also *make* math. A look at individual mathematicians invites children to wonder about their clever minds that saw connections and patterns others had missed—the kind of intellect that finds numbers, patterns, and relationships in the everyday. How did the Pythagoreans discover the mathematical nature of harmonics? Legend has it they plucked at different lengths of string. How did Descartes invent the Cartesian coordinates? Supposedly he watched a fly crawl up the wall and figured out how to calculate its location by imagining a grid and then pinpointing the fly on an intersection in the grid. Here is the kind of curiosity, observation, and adroit thinking we want to nurture in young people. Investigating these models helps.

One way for young people to attach math to its human origins is to make portraits of great mathematicians, each illustrated in terms of the concept he or she discovered or invented. Think of Descartes as a fly on the wall—an insect with Descartes's face and signature pageboy haircut. How about Pythagoras in his robe and sandals bouncing on a line? Humanizing invention and practice could also be done with all the great scientists, social scientists, and writers as well. Matteo Farinella's illustration of Santiago Ramón y Cajal is one example (refer to Figure 3.2).

Closing Thoughts on Math, Art, and Learning

Integrating math and art is far more than using math to make objects or compose paintings. Counting, measuring, drawing geometric shapes, and putting them together in structures are fine but only superficial ways to connect math to art. Indeed, these are just ways to *use* math in art or design, not to *understand* it through creative art-based inquiry. In this chapter I reviewed some concepts in mathematics that creative art-based inquiry and making art can illuminate, explained how artists explore math and its relationship to nature, and suggested more complex and current ways to think about math and connect it to art. My hope is that this discussion and the examples provided inspire a more substantive approach for educators to explore art and math together.

5

Social Studies
Understanding Ourselves and Others

WHAT ARE the social sciences? How do they relate to social studies? "Social studies" is the school subject that covers knowledge in the three branches of the social sciences: anthropology, sociology, and history, and their sister field, geography. Sociologists study social life—the various ways people interact and organize themselves. Anthropologists explore and describe cultural norms and forms of specific social groups. The two generally differ in their approach to their subjects. Sociology seeks to be objective and scientific, while anthropology embraces subjectivity in anthropological interpretation (Murphy, 1989). For its part, history analyzes and chronicles what has happened in the past. The subjects of history include people, events, places, situations, and the ideas and social forces that have shaped them. Finally, geography looks at how place, environment, and location affect the lives of people, and how people affect them.

FOUR DIMENSIONS OF SOCIAL STUDIES

To understand social studies, it is useful to look at them through Boix-Mansilla and Gardner's (1998) Four Dimensions of Understanding.

Purpose

Sociologists and anthropologists are interested in people. They aim to describe and understand cultural and social worlds. In doing so, they tell us about ourselves

and what influences our thinking and behavior. This includes the groups we belong to, the institutions that govern our lives, the cultural forms we embrace, and the beliefs we share. The social sciences have practical value. Knowing about social influences and structures and how they work helps us live in, participate in, and change those structures. The social sciences also satisfy a fundamental curiosity about who we are and why we are the way we are. They help us to understand

---

KEYS TO UNDERSTANDING

Some Questions in the Social Sciences, History, and Geography

- What are all the components of culture?
- How does culture shape an individual's sense of identity, values, ways of thinking and behaving, and worldview?
- How do individuals contribute to and change culture?
- How do humans organize, identify, and govern themselves?
- How are groups different? How are they alike?
- How does our location and natural environment influence us, and how do we affect them?
- How are we shaped by the people, events, and ideas that came before us?
- How do the images in art reflect a culture, its worldviews, and its times? How does art influence human thought?

---

ourselves and each other—the understanding we need to shape a better future together (Marshall, 2014).

Understanding ourselves also requires knowing our history—the social forces, people, ideas, and events that built the world we live in. For that reason, in schools, history falls under the umbrella of social studies. The same can be said of geography. Location and place are critical factors in the social and cultural world. A civilization's character and fate are often dependent on its geography (Knox & Martson, 2012).

Knowledge

Social Sciences. The knowledge of the social sciences divides into information about social life and the concepts that connect or explain these facts. This knowledge is vast; it covers the entire human world and all social experience. Today, researchers in both anthropology and sociology study life in our current globalized world, covering topics such as culture, socialization, social groups, and social change. Furthermore, they study humankind with the understanding that humans are complex beings whose behavior and lives are governed by personal, environmental, cultural, and social factors. Their knowledge is, by necessity, primarily provisional, context-based, and always emerging. Social researchers, therefore, shy away from making sweeping generalizations or developing general theories. They do, however, embrace some fundamental concepts, as follows:

- *Culture:* The combination of knowledge, beliefs, language, values, laws, customs, art, objects, and other capabilities and habits people have in a society
- *Social Construction of Reality:* The notion that culture shapes the way we think, conceptualize the world, and communicate our understandings
- *Cultural Relativism:* The idea that each culture has its own view of reality and, therefore, behavior or beliefs must be understood in the context of a culture; moreover, no culture has more validity than another
- *Identity:* The notion that identity is socially constructed

- *Change:* The idea that cultures and social realities transform over time
- *Globalization:* The integration of cultures and economies around the world, mostly under the influence of Western culture and capitalism (Kendall, 2012; Monaghan & Just, 2000; Murphy, 1989)

History. The discipline of history draws on a body of knowledge that ranges from discrete facts about historical figures and events to overarching theories about their meaning and significance. Important concepts in history are the following:

- *Pastness and Presentism:* The notion that the past is different from the present and that we must understand the past on its own terms and not impose present values on it
- *Stories and Facts:* The idea that history is a story created from and guided by facts. Historians may be inventive in how they report or interpret history, but they do not make things up.
- *Generalization and Specificity:* The notion that historians find general traits common to specific people, times, and events. These traits are the raw material of the theoretical narratives of history.
- *Chronology, Causation, and Meaning:* The idea that past phenomena influence or shape subsequent occurrences and understandings. Historians often look for specific causes for political, social, and cultural phenomena. By necessity, attribution of causation is primarily conjecture, because the relationship between cause and effect can be murky and indirect (Donahue & Drouin, 2014).

Geography. For geographers, the focus is on how geographic concepts inform and explain the forces that shape human life (Knox & Martson, 2012). These concepts include

- *Location:* Where something is situated
- *Space:* Where something is placed in relationship to other things

- *Scale:* The relative size of something
- *Place:* The meaning a site has for those who encounter it
- *Region:* A holistic understanding of a cluster of sites and an expanded notion of place
- *Movement:* The migration of human populations
- *Human–Environment Interaction:* Our collective impact on nature and its effect on living beings

Methods

Sociology. The social sciences use various methods for research. Sociology, for its part, employs four basic procedures. First, sociologists use surveys, which often include standardized interviews and questionnaires. Second, they analyze data gathered from sources such as public records, surveys, and official reports. The third method sociologists use, although less frequently, is experimentation. A fourth method is field studies. Through all of these methods, sociologists develop qualitative data that are often quantified.

Although sociology strives to maintain objectivity and scientific integrity, in qualitative social research, sociologists inch closer to the more subjective and interpretive anthropological approach to research. Whether quantitative or qualitative, a sociologist's aim is to be as objective, systematic, valid, and reliable as possible (Kendall, 2012).

Anthropology. In contrast to sociology, anthropology embraces a researcher's subjectivity. Anthropologists most often study smaller groups than sociologists do, and although they can use surveys and interviews, they frequently employ ethnographies—personal accounts that come from sustained, personal interaction between ethnographers and the people they study (Monaghan & Just, 2000). This relationship allows anthropologists to be fully immersed in a culture, to go deeply into cultural practices, and to be holistic in their thinking (Murphy, 1989). It also allows anthropology to be more like literature than a "hard" science. Anthropologists tell stories about their subjects and are known for penetrating and evocative

depictions called "thick description" (Geertz, 1973). In these ways, anthropologists build understandings of peoples that are richer and more in depth than are sociological statistical descriptions.

In summary, sociology aspires to an understanding of social trends and phenomena, while anthropology aims for a deeper understanding that can lead to empathy for others (Marshall, 2014).

History. For their part, historians draw on primary sources (documents created by the subjects of the research or documents created at the time under examination) and secondary sources (documents written afterward about the subject). Historians analyze these sources to reconstruct what happened and why. They revisit the past, tell stories, frame or generalize their findings, and in so doing, shape narratives or conceptual frames through which to understand the past and its relevance to the present (Donahue & Drouin, 2014).

Geography. In geographers' study of human life and its relationship to space, place, and environment, they employ many of the same qualitative and quantitative methods of other social scientists: surveys, ethnographies, diagrams, and graphs. Most important, since much of geographers' information concerns relative locations, configurations of places, human movement across spaces, and social phenomena in spaces, they convey information through maps of spaces and places (cartography) (Marshall, 2014).

Forms

The social sciences often construct and convey knowledge through verbal means in direct surveys and written reports of sociology, or more expressive forms such as stories and "thick descriptions" in anthropology. History, too, tends to be verbal in its storytelling, theories, and explanations. But all three domains also depend on visual forms (diagrams, tables, timelines, and documentaries) to relay information. Maps are also powerful tools for this, and geography often supports the social sciences and history with maps that locate, contextualize, and help convey information and tell stories.

INTERSECTION OF
SOCIAL STUDIES AND ART

Art always connects to social studies on the most basic level. Even if a piece of art is about jellyfish, fractal geometry, or imaginary animals, it is about a human or personal perspective on the subject. Art intersects with social studies in other ways as well:

- Art is a subject of social studies. Art and other forms of visual culture embody how cultural groups construct meaning and communicate it symbolically (Geertz, 1973). Whether the arts manifest in objects, images, dances, rituals, or drama, these forms are considered artifacts of social/cultural life (Prown, 2001). For that reason, anthropologists and historians study them to find out about a society's values, practices, and perspectives on the world.

- Social life is a subject of art. Many artists observe social phenomena closely and express their take on them in their artwork. Like sociologists, they often make the familiar "strange." That is, artists present subjects in ways that draw attention to them and prompt viewers to see them in a new light.

- Anthropology uses visual imagery and technology to gather information and to convey information. Anthropology's reliance on visual imagery for capturing information goes back to the beginnings of the discipline, when researchers sketched their subjects, their artifacts, and their activities. Today, visual anthropologists, who bring artistic skill and artistry to their scholarship, use visual means, particularly photography and video, to convey ideas; give their audiences a primary experience that makes the subject accessible and lively; and enable the subjects of the study to speak for themselves.

- Anthropology and contemporary art intersect in utilizing both current visual culture and historic imagery. While anthropology employs cultural images as artifacts or evidence, contemporary art appropriates these artifacts to change audience perception of them, to express ideas (with artifacts as metaphors), or to make social commentary (Marshall, 2014).

- Many contemporary artists use the tools, forms, and visual symbols of cartography to make and convey ideas. Artists may map places, but they are not bound to geography in the narrow sense of the word. Instead, they play with the metaphors inherent in geography to represent abstractions such as ideas, concepts, and emotions. To convey these metaphors, artists often create maps (Harmon, 2004).

- Art reimagines history. This is true in both Western and Asian art traditions. History paintings, for example, were long considered the premier art form in Europe after the Enlightenment. Artists illustrated historical figures and events often with great flair and imagination. Unlike historians, who were tethered to the "facts," artists could and did embellish, reinterpret, and mythologize historical events, stories, and people to unearth cultural "truths"—to promote the narratives behind history or to disclose and critique them (Keller, 2015). This tradition of revisiting history and mining it for what it means for the present is alive today. We find this primarily in the work of artists who explore history through examining and interpreting historic sites—often making art out of or in these sites (Keller, 2015).

- Art critiques sociology, anthropology, and historical narratives to help us understand the downsides of the social sciences. Art targets sociologists' scientific and statistical orientation, which tends to boil complex phenomena down to generalities and simple statistically significant factors, and it critiques anthropology for its tendency to exoticize, aestheticize, pigeonhole, and frame non-Euro-American cultures. Art also critiques historical narratives that benefit the powerful or focus primarily on wars, big political events, and heroes, neglecting the stories and realities of everyday life (Marshall, 2014).

- Art and anthropology merge to create hybrid art forms. New Genre Public Art (Lacy, 1995) and Art/Anthropology (Schneider & Wright, 2010) are two examples of art genres that began when artists turned their attention and art making toward social concerns. In these forms of art, artists enter communities to do ethnographic research as a basis for their artworks and then create visual or performative "post-studio" works that reflect the culture and life of the host community. These works not only push the boundaries of art, but they also build empathy for others and a sense of community among participants (Marshall, 2014).

- Art takes action. Socially engaged artists go beyond research, critique, and empathy to actively intervene and make social change. Since the 1960s, many artists have made art a form of social action. One example of social action and community-building comes to us from New Genre Public Art. *Code 33: Emergency Clear the Air!* (1997–1999) by Suzanne Lacy, Unique Holland, and Julio Morales was a massive performance on a garage rooftop in Oakland, California, in which 100 police officers and 150 young people told each other their stories and had deep discussions about pressing issues of authority and power, crime and safety, while groups of neighborhood people roamed among the discussion circles to listen (Lacy, ND).

Code 33 is now history, but its legacy lives on in a growing movement of social activism art. Today, socially engaged artists work in communities, make provocative or playful interventions (yarn-bombing and shop-dropping), create participatory public art, design and grow community gardens, construct eco-friendly environmental art, and create street art—and they teach. Teaching, whether art or any other subject, is now considered among many artists to be their artform—a way they can use their skills, knowledge, and creativity to help others learn and to make social change.

EXAMPLES OF ART EXPLORING CONCEPTS IN SOCIAL STUDIES

In this section I discuss six works to illustrate how contemporary art addresses significant concepts in social studies.

KEYS TO UNDERSTANDING

Crossovers/Intersections of Social Studies and Art

- Art and social studies focus on people and the human experience.
- Art is the subject of anthropology, history, and art history. Art serves as evidence and symbolic representation of culture, values, aesthetics, worldviews, mythologies, and social and personal life in anthropology and history.
- Art illustrates and reimagines history, often mythologizing and/or memorializing historical figures and events.
- Art critiques historical narratives, predominant social systems, power, and other significant concepts in the social world. It critiques the social disciplines as well.
- Art rises beyond critique to intervention, community building, and social action.

Artists and Social Scientists, Historians, and Geographers

- Social scientists and artists do research into social life and culture.
- Artists and anthropologists bring personal interpretation, embellishment, and lyricism to their studies.
- Social scientists and artists study and comment on human experience and the causes and effects of worldviews and other cultural factors.
- Artists use the methods and forms of social studies and history to research social phenomena and make commentary; they use forms such as maps to illustrate metaphors of the social and personal "worlds."

Identity in a Global World

Having grown up in Nigeria and emigrated to the United States as a young adult, Njideka Akunyili Crosby is an artist with a dual identity; she is both Nigerian and American. Her large but intimate painting/collages convey her bifocal perspective on life in powerful images reminiscent of the visual storytelling

FIGURE 5.1. Njideka Akunyili Crosby, *"The Beautyful Ones" Series #4* (2015)

traditions of African American art (Romare Bearden, Kerry James Marshall, Benny Andrews, and Jacob Lawrence are examples). In her artwork, Akunyili Crosby portrays her life in Los Angeles and contrasts it with her home in Nigeria.

For example, Akunyili Crosby's series of portraits of Nigerian girls titled *The Beautyful Ones* pictures girlhood in Nigeria. Figure 5.1 portrays a girl in her confirmation dress, attired for the rite of passage in the Christian church that denotes a girl's coming of age. Next to the girl is a blue plastic doll. While it may seem unremarkable, this figure holds a great deal of meaning and sets up a tension in the artwork. The doll is a contemporary version of an African power figure. This portrait makes one wonder. Is the image about the complexity of Nigerian culture and spirituality and the effects of colonization? Or is it about female

identity? Could this young girl be a power figure herself?

Cultural Artifacts and Meaning

In a current series of mixed media sculptures, Michael Rakowitz reconstructs 7,000 artifacts that were looted from the National Museum of Iraq at the beginning of the Iraq War (see the example in Figure 5.2). Rakowitz expresses his profound connection to his Iraqi roots and Iraqi life today by making the priceless stolen or destroyed artwork out of modern-day Iraqi commercial packaging materials. In doing so, he addresses the power historic objects have in sustaining cultural identity and how damaging their loss is to the people who inherited and treasure them. These recreations also speak of how difficult it is to capture what has been lost.

Historical Lens

Wendy Red Star challenges conventional thinking around the ways indigenous images have been portrayed through the colonial lens, and she reveals missing information with facts and details that have been

FIGURE 5.2. Michael Rakowitz, from *The Invisible Enemy Should Not Exist* (2007–ongoing)

FIGURE 5.3. Wendy Red Star, *Peelatchiwaaxpáash / Medicine Crow (Raven),* from *The 1880 Crow Peace Delegation Series* (2014)

erased in American history. The dual portrait in Figure 5.3 is of Peelatchiwaaxpáash / Medicine Crow (Raven), an important leader and visionary to the Apsáalooke Nation. This image is from a series on historic representations of Apsáalooke chiefs in which Red Star alters photographs by Charles Milton Bell (1848–1893), who was commissioned by the Bureau of Indian Affairs in Washington, DC. The original portraits altered here by Red Star were part of a series of delegation portraits Bell made of Apsáalooke leaders when they traveled to Washington, DC, in 1880 on a mission to attain peace and preserve their community. Red Star annotates these iconic photos with an overlay of texts that explain the meaning of the symbolic clothing worn by the chiefs. Through identifying these important articles of clothing, Red Star tells their stories. She also reveals the names of the *bachee-itche,* the Apsáalooke word for "chief," meaning "good man," portrayed in the photographs. In this way, she reminds the viewer that the *bacheeitche* were human beings who lived real lives.

Telling History

The history, everyday life, and mythology of the Sami people of northern Sweden are illustrated in simple, yet detailed, elegant embroidery by Sami artist Britta Marakatt-Labba. Figure 5.4 is from Marakatt-Labba's 24-foot-long horizontal embroidered scroll titled *History.* This subtle, delicate, yet monumental work spans Sami history, drawing a visible timeline from prehistory to the present. Along the line are vignettes of Arctic life: herding reindeer and fishing, driving snowmobiles, and living in tiny villages. The scroll

FIGURE 5.4. Britta Marakatt-Labba, *History* (2003–2007)

also tells of one pivotal event in Sami history: the Kautokeino Uprising, when the Sami people rebelled against foreign powers, such as the church and outside business owners, whom the Sami deemed exploitative and destructive to their culture and way of life. This is an historical and cultural record, told not by an historian but by an artist who lives with and within the history of her people.

Cartography of Information

Paula Scher paints exuberant, highly intricate maps covered with words in dense, flowing patterns of information. While her work resembles time-honored folk art traditions, Scher's maps are about contemporary issues, most frequently the menace of information overload. Figure 5.5 pictures another looming problem: the extreme weather patterns in the United States due to climate change. We see in Scher's map how exquisite images can delight the viewer while they deliver a chilling message.

Social Space and Living Social Commentary

Stephanie Syjuco is interested in issues of economy and labor. Many of her interactive works speak to concerns about commerce and consumerism. For example, her work *Money Factory* (see Figure 5.6) addresses economic issues that are particularly problematic for young people in Taiwan: the high cost of living and the uncertain future that it creates. Not an ordinary, static installation meant to be simply observed, *Money Factory* is instead a "crafting space" in the National Taiwan Museum of Fine Arts, where young people cut and pasted artificial money to create new money. We see them in this photograph making new money together as a game, a social event, and as an act of communal labor. The concepts of labor and making money were expressed further in the stacks of "money" that accrued as the youth produced them.

FIGURE 5.5. Paula Scher, *USA Extreme Weather* (2015)

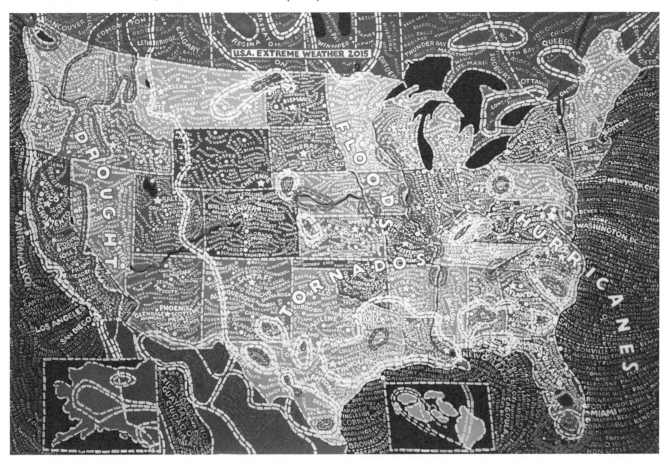

FIGURE 5.6. Stephanie Syjuco, *Money Factory (An Economic Reality Game), Taiwan Biennial* (2015)

INTEGRATING SOCIAL STUDIES AND ART IN THE CLASSROOM

How can children learn about social studies? One way is to simply directly study the ideas, issues, systems, and institutions that shape our collective lives. Another way is to tell the tales of people in the past who shaped today's institutions, values, social life, and cultures, or to tell the stories of people who are doing so today. Both approaches have their merits, and we need both of them. Perhaps, however, we need something more: art.

When we look at the artwork discussed in this chapter and think of its implications for teaching and learning, we can recognize how art can tell and embellish stories, and how art can enhance and invigorate scholarship. Indeed, art offers many entryways into social concerns and concepts—ways that enable young people to explore social life and forces personally and collectively, ways that are true to art and great for learning.

In making art about topics, young people can apply and build their knowledge; they can explore topics thoroughly and come up with their own interpretations. Art also invites young people to actively convey their knowledge and develop their own ideas. Moreover, it invites them to use cultural symbols and memes to do so. In observing and using symbols and icons in art, young artists can become more culturally literate; they learn about the "visual languages" of culture and how to use symbolism, style, imagery, and visual metaphors to make meaning.

Most important, art offers vehicles for young students to learn and think about difficult and controversial issues. Indeed, art can provide the most comfortable environment and best methods for youngsters to address serious, often daunting social problems and issues. This is because art can be indirect; it can enter into problems without being heavy-handed. Making art helps children grapple with issues in ways that are clever, subtle, oblique, and playful—ways that are amenable to them. Furthermore, at its most creative, art can motivate young learners and engage them in inventing imaginative solutions to problems, large or small, personal or cultural.

The examples I have presented are a small sample of the creative, playful, and subtle ways art addresses

KEYS TO UNDERSTANDING

Creative Art-Based Inquiry into Social Studies

- Address the core concepts of social studies through creative inquiry methods such as research into the concepts and their manifestations, observational drawings and sculpture, imaginative interpretations of information and concepts, and invention based on information and concepts.
- Use the methods and forms of the social sciences to explore and convey in art the concepts through research methods and presentation methods such as diagramming, mapping, and charting.
- Look at the disciplines of social sciences, history, and geography as active areas of inquiry that continue to construct and revise knowledge.
- See and explore the content of the disciplines in ways practicing researchers in the social sciences, history, geography, and artists do.
- Explore concepts through hands-on experiences, direct observation of concrete manifestations of those concepts, and play with ideas that stem from them. Make the connection between concepts and instances explicit and accessible to learners.
- Study social scientists, historians, cartographers, and geographers to follow and ascertain how they came to their research methods, analysis, and insights. Study the origin, history, and development of these disciplines.

serious Big Ideas in social studies, history, and culture. Try some of these strategies in teaching your social studies curriculum. When you do, address the concepts of social studies in the art projects and in the reflections that accompany them. Try not to copy exactly what these artists have done but adapt the essence of their approaches or ideas to your curriculum and to the interests of your learners. Above all, take from these artists their dispositions toward exploration, play, humor, honesty, and thoughtfulness. Exploring the social world and all its richness and difficulties can be artful and imaginative.

6

Language Arts
Creative Writing and Storytelling

WHY is creative writing, particularly story-telling, essential to learning? The language arts are at the core of the curriculum. Knowing how to read, write, and articulate ideas and knowledge are basic to learning and living a fulfilled life. Indeed, literacy is such a core concern in education that developing literacy is part of the curriculum in all subjects and not isolated to reading and writing classes.

The centrality of the language arts is reflected in the Common Core State Standards (CCSS) (Common Core State Standards Initiative, 2014), which focus on the language arts and mathematics, a sister "language" of numbers and relationships. The CCSS in English Language Arts has four principal tenets:

- Practice with complex texts
- Reading, writing, and speaking grounded in evidence, both literary and informational
- Building knowledge through content-rich nonfiction
- Use of language across the curriculum

While not dismissing the standards, in this chapter on the language arts my focus is on what is missing in them: creative writing and storytelling. I do this for the following reasons. First, with their concentration on expository writing and making clear and concise arguments, the CCSS slight the creative and imaginative branch of the language arts. For those of us who find creative activity to be a key way to learn, this is a serious omission. I try to fill that gap in this chapter.

Second, children learn through stories—the ones they hear and the ones they tell. This love of stories makes creating them and listening to them more natural ways to acquire and practice language skills, to learn how to sequence points and to build toward a climax or conclusion—skills one needs to make arguments and do expository writing. Storytelling, therefore, could be a pathway to fulfilling the standards.

Third, I concentrate on creative writing because it is an art form closely linked to and often an integral part of the visual and performing arts. As a mode of inquiry, creative writing, like the other arts, can roam freely across the curriculum to play with ideas and information housed in the other domains. Creative writing is in many ways the verbal equivalent of the visual and performing arts when it comes to curriculum integration. Through it, young people can make new, inventive, and surprising connections across the curriculum, personalize knowledge, and dig deeper into the meaning of information and ideas. This occurs through imaginative narratives, inventive use of language, projections beyond the literal, and elaborations on ideas and themes that creative writing encourages.

FOUR DIMENSIONS OF CREATIVE WRITING

As Rick Ayers (2014) suggests, creative writing is a vast and slippery domain—more an open-ended endeavor in thinking, emotion, narrative, imagination, and sensory experience than a strict discipline with rules and guidelines. Ayers alludes to the notion that many creative writers begin their work without a plan; they let the characters, narrative, or words lead the way. They get into a "flow" (Csikszentmihalyi, 1996) and allow their stories, ideas, and thoughts pour out of them onto the page. All creative writers do not work alike, however. While some writers allow their writing to lead them, some have loose outlines before they write, and some have their projects figured out beforehand. Organized or not, writers usually have intention and, therefore, have some idea where they are going (Turchi, 2004).

One thing all writers do is use words. Although, words have meaning and beauty in themselves, words are only the building blocks of writing. A creative writer takes words and shapes them into a form— a poem, a story, an essay, an epic novel, or a simple sentence—and it is through these forms that meaning flows and accumulates. To dive deeper into creative writing, I will look at it through the lens of Boix-Mansilla and Gardner's (1998) Four Dimensions of Understanding.

Purpose

Why do we write? First, we write to learn. Writing captures our wordless thoughts and experiences and restores them to consciousness by attaching them to words (an idea from Caroline Marshall discussed in Ayers, 2014, p. 131). That is, words enable us to realize our tacit knowledge. Writing, therefore, is how writers learn from themselves. This often occurs organically throughout the writing process. Furthermore, writing is a form of creative inquiry. It involves research into a subject, whether it is ourselves or an "outside" topic, through creative processes, and allows us to explore knowledge and probe further into it in an open and improvisational way (Ayers, 2014).

Audiences also learn. Writing takes what is interior and private and makes it exterior and public (Ricoeur, 1991). When knowledge and ideas go public and touch an audience, the audience interprets them, connects them to themselves, and learns from them.

Second, we write to travel (Turchi, 2004). Creative writing, particularly stories, takes a writer and reader into places they could otherwise never be able to go—

into the mind of a narrator or over the moon; out on an adventure in an imaginary land or into the inner sanctum of Marie Antoinette's palace; cruising through the bloodstream or floating on an ancient ship. Creative stories can introduce us to people we would never meet and let us experience events long past. Stories can take us into the heart and soul of an author, into our own heads, or into outer space. The places stories can take us, and the experiences and knowledge they can give us, spark our imagination and inspire us to keep traveling. In a nutshell, creative storytelling expands our experience.

This leads to the third purpose of creative writing and storytelling: to create empathy. Stories bring "others" to life; they help readers to see others in full and in intimate detail, to undertake their experiences and struggles, and to enter into their thoughts, emotions, and dreams. While storytelling, in particular, helps us understand others and care about them, it also generates concern about issues and ideas by giving them a human face and revealing their implications and effects. In short, a good story told in rich language and detail can make what seems abstract and removed into something concrete, immediate, and compelling.

Knowledge

The knowledge of creative writing is the territory a writer explores. It is a mix of personal knowledge and perspective with information and ideas germane to the topic at hand (Ayers, 2014). Writers often do research to gather knowledge of the subject they write about and, then, in the process of writing, create new knowledge about a topic as they connect information and ideas, shape narratives, and invent and embellish characters and events. A good example of this is historical novels, which blend researched facts and information with imaginative embellishments to breathe life into historical figures, times, and events. Knowledge in these stories begins with information about real occurrences and people and is extended and deepened by what the facts imply. An irony here lies in how the fictive aspects of a novel—the projections and elaborations on the "facts"—often reveal greater truths than the "facts" alone (Ricoeur, 1991).

KEYS TO UNDERSTANDING

Some Questions in Creative Writing and Storytelling

- How do we express in words and literary forms our ideas, feelings, experiences, hopes, and fantasies?
- How and what do we learn from writing—about ourselves and the world outside ourselves?
- How does creative writing take us to places beyond our reach (into other worlds and into the minds of others)?
- How do stories create empathy for others and motivate us to care about phenomena outside ourselves and our experience?
- How does writing generate one's own thinking and reflection and allow a writer to communicate with others?
- How do words allow us to capture slippery ideas? How do they help us to remember, revisit, and relive ideas and experiences?
- How does evocative language and compelling narrative make abstract concepts lively, relevant, and engaging?

Methods

Peter Turchi (2004) discusses in metaphorical terms how writers write. He likens creative writing to exploring and mapping, with the realm of the writer as territory to be discovered, explored, and mapped. Following his metaphor, Turchi claims that writing entails two separate but complementary acts. One act is *exploration*, or venturing into unknown territory, and the other act is *presentation*, or shaping a work. The act of exploration is open-ended and often chaotic; the act of presentation imposes order on that chaos. Turchi likens presentation to mapping. Exploration and presentation occur simultaneously and interdependently until presentation takes the upper hand and a "product" is realized. This means that writers map the territory as they create it. The tension and symbiosis between exploration's open-endedness and play and presentation's imposition of order and form

is universal in the arts and creative inquiry. It is how the creative process works.

Creative writers have a myriad of ways of exploring and mapping, and it is difficult to pin down a general methodology (Ayers, 2014). Some brave folks try, however. Clark (2016), for instance, argues that writing has five steps: idea, collect, focus, draft, and clarify (p. 241). Like other formulas for complex processes (Wallas's [2014] four stages of creative process, for example), Clark's simple formula gives us some insight into writing but does not account for the complex meandering, iterative, and evolving nature of any creative process, writing included.

Clark (2016) does, however, provide some guidance in the craft of writing and storytelling. He lists a number of strategies writers use to convey ideas and/or push a narrative. These include basic formal strategies such as juxtaposing ideas or imagery to build contrast, repeating words and phrases to create rhythm, building the plot toward a crescendo, and going into detail to give specificity and texture to a story. A quick perusal of these strategies reveals that many of them echo the creative conceptual strategies of contemporary visual art (see Chapter 7), in particular, metaphor, juxtaposition, elaboration, extension, transformation, and projection.

One strategy in writing and art that deserves particular attention here is the juxtaposition of two extremes of "distance" (Hart, 2011): the close-up and the panoramic overview. The close-up is a rich description of character, plot, and place in details that make a story juicy. The overview is abstractions that sum up these details, put them in perspective, and connect them to a bigger picture. These two extremes of close and far-away rest on the opposite ends of the Ladder of Abstraction (Hayakawa, 1939). The ladder consists of various levels of concrete and abstract, with the concrete or close-up on the bottom rung of the ladder and progressing up the ladder to the abstract or panoramic on the top. Both Hart and Hayakawa argue that good writing requires directly connecting and juxtaposing the two extremes rather than lingering on the murky middle rungs between them. For example, a discussion about an abstract concept like creative brilliance requires juxtaposing it with concrete examples, such as Lin-Manuel Miranda's musical *Hamilton* or Julie Taymor's costume and set designs for *The Lion King*. I focus on the Ladder of Abstraction here because it relates to a primary theme of this book: the connection of concrete entities to abstract ideas as a primary trait of creativity (Necka, 1986) and as a key to learning in art making (J. H. White, personal communication, New York, March 2017).

Writers use other creative strategies that are more process oriented. They include researching source material; mapping out plots and points before a writer begins writing or as they write; revisiting, revising, and reorganizing the text; accumulating details and connections to other things along the way; and editing out what does not belong or work. Evidence of these strategies is not apparent in the final text; they are how the text is written and takes shape.

Forms

As mentioned before, creative writing comes in many forms. They range from poetry, such as haiku, epic poems, sonnets, and free-form poetry such as rap; to storytelling in novels, novellas, memoires, biographies, folk tales, and short stories; to descriptive essays, letters, plays, screenplays, song lyrics, and opera librettos.

KINDS OF STORIES

There are many ways to tell a story, and many kinds of stories to tell. Here I concentrate on two kinds of stories: creative nonfiction and magic realism. Why these two genres? Both of them are grounded in reality while they also entail imagination and artistry. They are, therefore, good vehicles for conveying "facts" or curriculum content to young learners. Moreover, both are literary ways to practice creative inquiry and creative thinking skills.

Creative Nonfiction

Creative nonfiction is practiced by journalists, history writers, biographers, memoirists, and anyone who wants to take nonfiction beyond the cold hard facts to the human side of the story. Writer Lee Gutkin (2012) defines creative nonfiction as "true stories well told"

(p. 6). What makes these stories nonfiction is that they always adhere to the truth. This truth may be in the eye of the author, but creative nonfiction writers do not make things up. What makes these stories creative is the way the writer conceives ideas, sums up circumstances, portrays personalities, describes places, and forms and presents information. The task of the writer is to make the real "strange," to tell it in a way that grabs the attention of the readers and compels them to see the subject differently. Another task is to tell true stories in the most captivating, vibrant, and powerful ways possible. To do this, creative nonfiction writers apply the literary craft of poets, playwrights, and fiction writers (Gutkin, 2012).

Creative nonfiction lends itself to children's learning because it remains true to the subjects children study, while it allows them to explore, convey, and embellish information in spirited literary ways—in artful poetic and descriptive language, dynamic action, and copious attention to detail. Furthermore, writing creative nonfiction exercises a child's imagination: It requires the creative strategies we find in all the arts, particularly elaboration (embellishing the information), projection (entering the minds, worlds, and lives of the characters or speculating what could happen based on what is already there), and transforming a straightforward narrative into a form that engages its audience with the content.

Magic Realism

Magic realism also uses colorful imagery and style to tell a story. However, in magic realism, the story wanders into fantasy, and fantasy fuses seamlessly with reality. We see this fusion in the novels of Colombian author Gabriel García Márquez, whose *One Hundred Years of Solitude* (1970) is the classic example of magic realism. In this sinuous tale of many generations of a Colombian family, a character's ancestors hover in the shadows; gypsies mysteriously appear and reappear in magical caravans; and a young girl rises upward, never to be seen again. While fancies such as these weave through the story, taking the reader into a dreamlike state of mind, the novel treats these leaps beyond reality not as fictions or illusions but as real events. Although filled with imaginary people and happenings, magic realism has a ring of truth. Indeed, it is called magic *realism* because it plays with fantasy to get at a deeper reality—the interior reality of the mind, where beliefs, memories, thoughts, and ideas are real.

Also, the fantasy of magic realism is deeply metaphorical. Reality is couched in metaphors. In *One Hundred Years of Solitude*, the ancestors are the past that is forever hovering over the living. The gypsies are knowledge born of freedom and shrouded in mystery—they know the secrets of the outside world that the village locals can barely fathom. The little girl is the soul—the essence behind the façade of a living person. In transforming her into a spirit, García Márquez tells us the girl is not *like* a spirit, she *is* one.

Magic realism arose out of the literary world of Latin America, where its underlying purpose was, and still is, to compel the reader to doubt what is considered real—particularly the social, cultural, psychological, and emotional realities that keep people in their place. The ultimate goal of magic realism is to introduce readers to new possibilities and new existences. It does this by probing and disrupting reality. In the Latin America where it began, magic realism is a social/political instrument for raising consciousness, which can ultimately lead to social change (Bowers, 2004; Leal, 1995).

Much of its creativity—and power—lies in the way magic realism uses metaphor. Because it is metaphorical, magic realism is a powerful tool young learners can employ to get at "truths" and to create stories that explore them. That is because using metaphors allows learners to embody ideas and knowledge in tangible things. Metaphors also generate ideas. They call up associations and invite a young writer to follow those associations, learn about their subject through those associations, and follow the implications through storytelling. An exploration of a metaphor can also provide a young writer with a subject for a story, an imaginative lens through which to view the subject and tell its story, and a rich trove of ideas and details that ground the story in real things and make the story compelling. Tell a story with and through metaphors and you have magic realism.

KEYS TO UNDERSTANDING

Crossovers and Intersections of Art and Creative Writing

- Creative writing/storytelling and the visual arts are imaginative artforms grounded in observation, experiences, and reality with the freedom to expand on them, embellish them, and project from them.
- Both reveal and convey inner and outer realities.
- Both rely on imagination for invention and insights.
- Both are ways we make meaning and come to understand. They are ways writers learn from themselves.
- Art and creative writing involve shaping "raw material" into compelling, meaningful, and artful forms.

Creative Writers and Artists

- Writers use creative strategies similar to those used in the other arts.
- Both artists and writers tell stories in imaginative, colorful, and lyrical ways.
- Both artists and writers embellish on and extend ideas to make ideas and topics come alive and be compelling.
- Both artists and writers connect abstract ideas to concrete specific characters, experiences, symbolism, metaphor, and detail.
- Writers and visual artists do research as preparation for art making or writing. The creative process is a form of research in both domains: It builds knowledge and understanding through thinking, imagination, invention, and creative process.

ART THAT TELLS STORIES

The visual arts have always told stories. From the first cave paintings, to illustrations of myths and legends, to history paintings of events, heroes, and royalty, to depictions of common everyday life, visual imagery has been used to pass on stories from generation to generation. Today, storytelling is alive and well in the visual arts. Graphic novels are a prime example. Another is the African American storytelling tradition, with its roots in story quilts and its contemporary incarnation in works by Faith Ringgold and two artists discussed here. In this section, I continue the examination of creative nonfiction and magic realism, and connect them to examples of visual art that correspond with these genres. An example of art that borders on pure fiction is also discussed.

Creative Nonfiction in Art

Benny Andrews tells true stories about African American life in dramatic, detailed, and evocative ways. Many of his paintings depict the history of African Americans—their community, family life, and struggles in the American South, where Andrews was born. In Andrews's work, we find a "true story well told" (Gutkin, 2012, p. 6). His style of simple stark colors and elongated figures connects his work to African American folk-art traditions. This austere style is particularly vivid and expressive; it compellingly projects pain, rage, and exhaustion as well as love, compassion, and dignity. In his *Migrant* series, Andrews depicts the African American migration from the American South in the early to mid-20th century to northern urban communities like Harlem in New York City. Figure 6.1 is Andrews's scene of 1930s Harlem, in which a newly arrived family, awestruck and uncertain, faces their strange new home and future.

Magic Realism in Art

While creative nonfiction embroiders reality with style, detail, and innovative storytelling, magic realism disrupts reality with surprising metaphorical imagery that poses provocative questions. Figure 6.2 is Mark Ryden's *The Apology* (2006)—an image in which Ryden's hyper-realistic style amplifies a vision of a young girl confronted with the melancholy gaze of an upended tree stump. This image questions the common notion of trees as inert and unconscious "things," compelling the viewer to see trees as sentient beings—vulnerable, soulful, and wise. Ryden's goal is to build empathy for defenseless life forms, and to do this, he uses illusion and metaphors. The tree could be nature with its eye representing wisdom and sorrow.

The little girl could be humankind—apologetic and sorrowful but ultimately passive.

Ryden's work is indicative of a very popular genre in contemporary art called Pop Surrealism. As a form of Surrealism, Pop Surrealism connects to the Surrealist movement in early to mid-20th-century European art, which also commented on reality by disrupting it with haunting, often dreamlike, nonsensical imagery.

In the same vein, Kerry James Marshall inserts dreamlike imagery into his storytelling paintings. In many of his works, he layers metaphorical imagery that represents his and the African American community's memories, beliefs, and hopes onto scenes from their lives. In *Souvenir II* (see Figure 6.3), Marshall enters the mind, memory, and living room of the woman he portrays. He makes memories and longing as tangible and material as the furniture. He does this by featuring a renowned "souvenir" of loss and hope, the tapestry portraying the two Kennedy brothers and Dr. Martin Luther King, Jr.; by giving his subject wings; and by placing a heavenly cloud filled with the spirits of departed loved ones on the ceiling above the woman's head.

Fiction in Art

My final example, Luigi Serafini's *Codex Seraphinianus* (1981/2013) (see Figures 6.4 and 6.5) is not creative nonfiction or magic realism. It is fiction pure and simple. That means it leaves reality behind, taking storytelling art a step further into fantasy. As a detailed and extensive tour of a miraculous land, the *Codex* is a visual encyclopedia that carries the reader to places where people, plants, animals, architecture, and objects are mysterious, colorful, and playful—and do things one would never expect. Figure 6.4 illustrates a machine that creates, twists, and ties rainbows. Figure 6.5 depicts trees escaping their rooted captivity and using their roots to propel themselves across the water. While Serafini's style is "realistic," his imagery is fanciful. The *Codex* is, therefore, a surreal puzzle. To add to the puzzlement, the *Codex* was inspired by another much earlier enigma: *The Voynich Manuscript*, an early 15th-century volume that has baffled scholars ever since it was first discovered.

To add to the mystery, the *Codex* is written in an indecipherable language that challenges the "reader"

FIGURE 6.1. Benny Andrews, *Harlem USA*, from the *Migrant* Series (2004)

FIGURE 6.2. Mark Ryden, *The Apology* (2006)

FIGURE 6.3. Kerry James Marshall, *Souvenir II* (1997)
© Kerry James Marshall, Courtesy of the artist and Jack Shainman Gallery, New York

to find meaning in a cryptic text. In this way, the *Codex* pokes fun at our expectations of language while it delights us with its cleverness. The *Codex* is a work of visual art in the form of a story or book (Serafini, 1981/2013). It is also a play on the convention of ethnography. Above all, it is a great example of how creative projection and elaboration work to accumulate meaning and push a clever idea further to yield ever more whimsical and imaginative results.

LITERACY THROUGH VISUAL ART

Visual art helps build literacy skills—both verbal and visual. In regard to visual literacy, although it is commonly argued that the visual arts are a universal lan-

guage, art is most often culturally specific in style, imagery, and symbolism, and therefore, only partially universal. Art does, however, often express universal experiences, values, and themes in culturally specific ways. Thus, young learners from many backgrounds and cultures can respond to visual imagery on their own terms. They can grasp what they relate to and, over time, develop visual literacy—learn to recognize new visual symbols and memes and decipher their meaning. Just think what children might learn about cultural symbols when they explore the imagery in Kerry James Marshall's *Souvenir II* or Benny Andrews's *Harlem USA*.

Visual art can also help develop language skills. Looking at art invites second language learners and young children who are learning to read and write to

FIGURE 6.4. Manipulation of Rainbows: Pages from Luigi Serafini's *Codex Seraphinianus* (1981/2013)

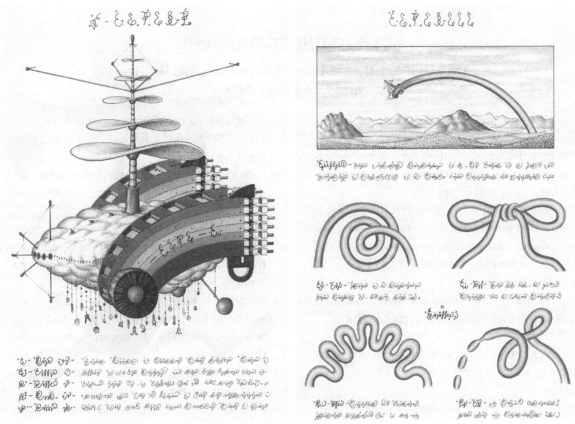

FIGURE 6.5. Escaping Trees: Pages from Luigi Serafini's *Codex Seraphinianus* (1981/2013)

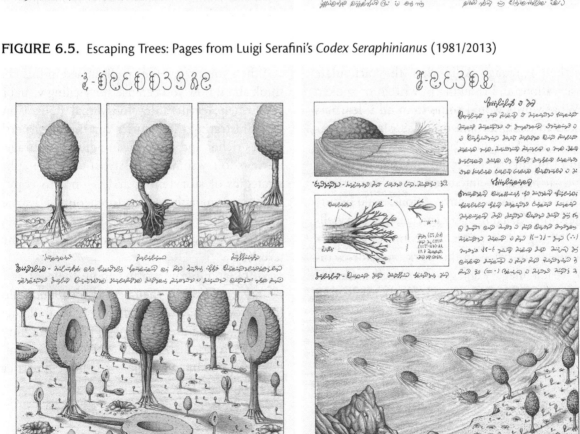

KEYS TO UNDERSTANDING

Creative Art-Based Inquiry into Creative Writing and Language Arts

- Use the methods and forms of the language arts, creative writing, and visual art to explore how they all use narrative, details, embellishment, and evocative imagery, style, and structure to make abstract ideas lively, "real," and compelling.
- Look at the disciplines of writing and storytelling as active areas of inquiry that continue to deepen our understanding of significant ideas and human experience. See and explore creative writing in the ways practicing writers do.
- Juxtapose and integrate visual and verbal. Use both modes to illustrate the same concepts and/or phenomena.
- Write titles, explanations, and reflections on visual imagery to attach, extend, and expand their meaning.
- Illustrate stories to practice visualization and concretize meaning.

- Build stories around visual imagery to explore and extend the meaning of the images and connect to them personally.
- Explore how writers and storytellers reflect and are shaped by their times, experiences, culture, and places they live or lived in.
- Investigate how writers and artists bring deep and fresh perspective to significant ideas and influence the culture and ideas of their times and future times.
- Study the history of writing, storytelling, poetry, and other literary forms across time and place, and how they dovetail with concurrent movements in the visual arts.
- Explore how creative writing/storytelling can be used with visual art to investigate, interpret, integrate, and bring imaginative personal interpretation to the academic domains.

practice their language skills when they articulate their observations and thinking in written or spoken words. What words would come to mind if learners were asked to decipher and describe Mark Ryden's *Apology* or Luigi Serafini's *Codex*? What skills—both verbal and thinking skills—could children acquire by forming their responses into questions, observations, and responses? What rich conversations could occur?

Furthermore, visual imagery can catalyze storytelling. Storytelling art, in particular, conjures stories—stories told by the artist in the work and stories inspired by visual imagery and generated in the mind of the viewer. Consider the stories learners might find embedded in the works described here or the stories they themselves could generate. The creative nonfiction art of Benny Andrews could inspire stories of lived experience. Magic realism and fiction art (Serafini's *Codex*) could instigate more imaginative tales.

When you review the art discussed in this chapter, think about how you can use storytelling visual imagery to help learners develop verbal skills. Consider how illustrating their stories can make learners' narratives richer and more meaningful. Encourage your learners to try some of the stylistic and metaphorical strategies of storytelling artists—not to copy their styles and metaphors, but to encourage learners to develop a style that fits their stories and a metaphor that takes their stories into new and more meaningful territory.

Think about how writing about their art can help young people clarify their artistic ideas and reflect on their processes. Above all, ponder how similar art and creative writing are as forms of creative inquiry and how, when braided together, they complement each other and can integrate the curriculum in particularly meaningful and creative ways.

PART III

Art-Based Strategies for Creative Inquiry

IN PART III, the discussion moves from foundations, ideas, and theories to practical and concrete ways to organize and implement creative thinking, creative art-based inquiry, and curriculum integration. Chapter 7 explains creative thinking and the tools and strategies that can be used for fostering creative inquiry and integrated learning in the classroom. Chapter 8 presents frameworks from Harvard University's Project Zero that teachers can use to think through, organize, and deepen their curriculum. Chapter 9 provides examples of trails of interconnected projects and learning experiences. Part III, therefore, is all about practical applications—frameworks, guidance, and ideas for implementation.

7

Learning Strategies for Creative Inquiry

THIS CHAPTER is about learning through creative thinking and making. It addresses questions such as: What is creative thinking? How do learners use creative thinking and methods to learn and build understanding? What tools can they use to propel their thinking? To answer these questions, I begin the chapter with notions of creative thinking and connect them to the multiple creative strategies contemporary artists use to conceptualize and convey their ideas. From there, I explain two of these strategies—metaphor and mapping—as creative strategies young people can use for learning and building understanding. The last part of the chapter describes the research workbook, a basic tool that supports and propels student learning through creative inquiry. The tools and strategies described here are "hybrids," procedures that blend pedagogical methods with creative strategies from contemporary art.

KINDS OF CREATIVE THINKING

Ritchhart (2015) maintains that we learn through thinking. By this he suggests that, to learn in any meaningful way, we must mull over a subject, interpret it, and digest it. We must consider its implications as thoroughly as we can; we must think critically. Thinking, therefore, generates and is an integral part of learning. This suggests that mimicking and memorizing, which may be part of a learning experience, are not enough.

What about thinking in inquiry? One value of an inquiry is its emphasis on thinking, particularly the complex thinking entailed in asking questions, analyzing a subject, generalizing about it, and applying knowledge to solve problems. This thinking is linear and logical thinking, and it is essential to inquiry. What about creative inquiry? The thinking in creative inquiry is even more complex. As discussed in Chapter 1, creative inquiry is powered by *poietic logic,* the interweaving of logical and linear thinking with associative and nonlinear thinking. Poietic logic is another term for *creative thinking.* It is the force in creative inquiry that propels learning into new territory—to revelations and understandings that strict logic and analysis cannot reach.

The question arises: What exactly is creative thinking? Although creativity can be a slippery phenomenon, which many believe defies analysis and definitions, there are theories that make creative thinking (a major part of creativity) less ill-defined, less difficult to pin down. Cognitive scientists, in particular, provide clear descriptions of creative thinking. For example, Finke, Ward, and Smith (1996) define creative thinking as conceptual combination (merging concepts to create a new one) and conceptual expansion (enlarging a concept's web of associations). Kirst and Dickmeyer (1973/1992) identify many kinds of creative thinking, some of which reveal its logical aspects:

- Analyzing (examine and evaluate information and ideas)
- Elaborating (build on or add details to a concept, entity, or information)

- Associating (see connections among concepts and entities)
- Constructing (build physical objects and/or conceptual structures)
- Translating (convey ideas in different forms or modalities)
- Producing (make sense; make a coherent thought out of lots of thoughts and ideas)
- Revising (rework an idea or way the idea is conveyed; find new connections or ways of perceiving)

Necka (1986) adds similar types of creative thinking:

- Forming associations
- Recognizing similarities
- Constructing metaphors
- Transforming (change or morph something into something new)

Necka (1986) also identifies "seeing the abstract in the concrete" as creative thinking. This capacity to find the abstract in concrete entities—to see how something represents or embodies a concept—is emphasized in this book because it is the core of learning in general (see Chapters 4 and 5) and it is a big part of art-based thinking and making art. But finding the abstract is just the beginning. After an artist deciphers an abstract concept behind a concrete phenomenon, they translate the concept into a visual form—an artwork that embodies and conveys that abstract concept. Art educator John Howell White (personal communication, New York, March 2017) stresses this transition from concrete to abstract and back to concrete as the key to conceptualizing and constructing meaningful artworks and learning from them. The process continues when the artist and viewers of the work find the abstract concept (with the added value of the artist's interpretation) in the artwork (see Figure 7.1). On both the artist's and the viewers' parts, the artwork is a vessel for an abstract concept and a vehicle for understanding it.

CREATIVE STRATEGIES IN CONTEMPORARY ART

Just as art makes abstract concepts visible in tangible visual forms, contemporary art often makes creative thinking visible. It does this by displaying the creative strategies artists use to manifest ideas in their artworks. What are creative strategies? How do they differ from creative thinking? Creative strategies are creative thinking taken to the next step; they are specific ways artists (or anyone creating) manipulate materials, imagery, and forms to conceptualize and create their artworks. In a nutshell, creative strategies are creative thinking put into action. These strategies are also called conceptual strategies because they are ways to realize and communicate ideas.

Reasons for Identifying Creative Strategies

Why should we pay attention to creative strategies? We do this to demystify creativity. Taking the mystery out of creativity (at least some of it) is a good thing. It does not diminish the value of creativity or the delight we take in it. To the contrary, it opens creativity up to everyone and it sparks our own creative thinking. Much contemporary art helps demystify creativity because the creative strategies we find in contemporary art are accessible, doable techniques young people can use to come up with ideas and to convey those ideas. Furthermore, when learners encounter a work of art, they can look for more than formal qualities, subject matter, and meaning but can also observe how that meaning was constructed. This adds a whole new dimension to critiquing art, whether it is one's own or someone else's. For example, looking at Dawn Ng's *Walter: Somewhere Over a Concrete Rainbow* (see Figure 7.2), one can readily see the use of juxtaposition, change of scale, and use of unusual materials.

And there are other reasons for identifying creative strategies: First, there are a variety of strategies, and they present multiple ways to manipulate imagery to make meaning. Knowing the strategies gives young artists many possibilities and ideas for making meaning in their artwork. When they are "stuck" and don't know how to proceed, they can play with and use these learned strategies.

Second, in creative inquiry, learners can apply a creative strategy here and there to move their inquiry in unexpected directions, to play with artistic meaning making, to build on and transform given knowledge into something new, to see knowledge differently, and to make new and meaningful connections.

FIGURE 7.1. Map of the Concrete–Abstract Trail

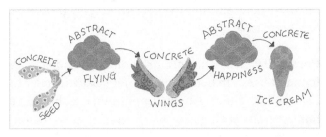

Third, many creative strategies come naturally to young people. Integrating them into a learning experience or project taps into what they already do and helps them to sustain and grow their innate playfulness and creativity. It does this by honoring what they do and giving young learners the support they need to go further.

Fourth, identifying and naming these strategies also helps learners to develop a "metacognitive vocabulary"—words they can use to describe what they do. This can make their reflections more about process and less about evaluating whether they like or dislike a final product. Young learners can start building this vocabulary early on, and teachers can adjust the vocabulary to fit the age-group they teach.

Finally, an awareness of the creative strategies is also helpful for the teacher. It enables teachers to rec-ognize the strategies in learners' work and provides concrete indicators for assessing learners' creative thinking.

Examples of Creative Strategies

On the following pages I describe a variety of creative strategies and provide examples from contemporary art. This list comes from analyzing contemporary art and realizing some simple and concrete ways artists convey complex ideas. Notice how closely these strategies align with the kinds of creative thinking identified by cognitive scientists. Also, note how simple strategies can produce complex meaning, particularly when they are applied to images and objects that have meaning in themselves and resonate with viewers. Lastly, more than one strategy can be used in one artwork; when this is the case, they overlap and work together.

Change Scale. *Make an object larger or smaller in relationship to surrounding entities.* Dawn Ng plays with our sense of scale. For her many installations of *Walter,* she places giant inflatable versions of a toy rabbit in different locations. In Figure 7.2, a colossal Walter graces the central square of one of Singapore's

FIGURE 7.2. Dawn Ng, *Walter: Somewhere Over a Concrete Rainbow* (2010)

FIGURE 7.3. Joyce Hsu, *Incomplete Metamorphosis* (ND)

many housing complexes. Ng's sculptures bring a contemporary twist to the genre of art exemplified in the work of Claes Oldenberg, who created huge sculptures of common objects such as brooms, spoons, typewriter erasers, clothespins, and hamburgers. These pop art icons, produced in the 1960s, '70s, and '80s, grace many public spaces today.

Hybridize. *Combine multiple parts of things to create something new.* Amy Youngs, like other Bio Artists, works with live organisms to call attention to their natural processes and how humans manipulate them. Grafting one plant onto another is a common way botanists exploit a plant's capacity to bond with other plants to create new life forms. Youngs plays with that idea to build empathy for cacti; she grafts one cactus onto another or adds furry collars to make her cacti unique, surprising, and adorable (refer to Figure 2.7).

Joyce Hsu's delightful mechanical insects reflect a hybridization of machine and insect. Her *Incomplete Metamorphosis* (ND; see Figure 7.3) is one good

example of a futuristic, evolving hybrid bug. It is pictured here buzzing over Argonne Playground in San Francisco.

Personify. *See animals or inanimate objects in human terms.* In her *Cosmology for a Skeptic* (refer to Figure 2.1), Timea Tihanyi implies that rabbits have human traits such as curiosity, wonder, and reason. Her rabbits are philosophers, and reality is a house of cards teetering on a stack of books. This art poses some intriguing questions about certainty, knowing, and wondering—subjects that preoccupy thoughtful humans. Personification is a common strategy in children's literature. For example, recall the humanlike rabbits in classic children's books: The White Rabbit

FIGURE 7.4. Joan Brown, *The Bride* (1970)
© The Estate of Joan Brown, courtesy of George Adams Gallery, New York

FIGURE 7.5. Scott Musgrove, *The Late Fauna of Middle America* (2009). From *The Late Fauna of Early North America: The Art of Scott Musgrove* (Musgrove, 2009)

in *Alice in Wonderland* (Lewis Carroll); Brer Rabbit in *The Tales of Uncle Remus: The Adventures of Brer Rabbit* (Julius Lester); and Peter Rabbit in *The Tale of Peter Rabbit* (Beatrix Potter). Note also that the house of cards in Tihanyi's piece is a metaphor.

Elaborate. *Embellish.* Elaborating is common strategy in storytelling. Writers take an idea or a character and "flesh it out," that is, go into detail. They use descriptive, evocative language to bring their characters to life in the reader's imagination. In the visual arts, elaborating is often adding to or embellishing an idea or image. Joan Brown's *The Bride* (1969; see Figure 7.4) is an example of visual embellishment or elaboration. With an accumulation of vibrant detail and patterns, the lovely cat bride becomes animated, vivid, and full of personality. Notice that this is also an example of personification.

Scott Musgrove's work is another example of embellishment. In his book *The Late Fauna of Early North America* (2009), he embroiders his portraits of imaginary extinct animals with minute details and names, elaborate frames, illustrations of their habitats, and stories about them. A good example is *The Late Fauna of Middle America* (see Figure 7.5), a natural history-style illustration of where these imaginary beasts once lived.

Extend. *Push or follow ideas further.* When writers extend, they follow or take a character through a trail of events or experiences. Extension is, therefore, making a plot. Scott Musgrove uses the same strategy in his artwork. He addresses the issue of animal extinction by following a character through an elaborate story. Musgrove is the protagonist, who in the guise of a natural historian, bravely ventures into the wild behind strip malls and under parking lots to seek out and document the wildlife that once inhabited these sites. In these wild places, his character discovers the remains of imaginary extinct animals, which he "restores" and memorializes in his portraits of them (refer to Figure 2.8). In the end, Musgrove's bestiary and tales of "scientific" research make an extended satire on natural historians and natural history museums, along with a serious underlying message about animal extinction.

FIGURE 7.6. Bill Burns, from the *Safety Gear for Small Animals* Series (1994)

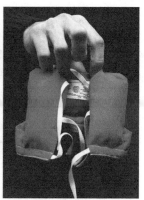

FIGURE 7.7. Ellen Jewett, *The White Stag* (2014)

Project. *Speculate about what could happen, identify with others, and imagine or envision what is not there based on what is there.* As speculation of what could happen, projection is the strategy behind science fiction. Scott Musgrove's book *The Late Fauna of Early North America* (2009) (refer to Figures 2.8 and 7.5) is a good example of projection that fantasizes like science fiction but is more like science fiction in reverse. That is, Musgrave speculates about what might have been. This is also a strategy that is employed in the scientific pursuits of paleontology and archaeology.

Projection can also be "walking in someone else's shoes." Bill Burns does this in his series of tiny safety gear designed to protect rodents and other small vulnerable creatures (see Figure 7.6). Here is an example of an artist projecting into the minds of animals, creating art that expresses empathy for these animals, and providing a solution to their problems.

Jane Hammond has another angle on projection. In *My Heavens* (2004; refer to Figure 2.2), Hammond's map of personal constellations, she addresses how humans search for patterns and underlying order in random natural phenomena—how they connect dots and imagine what is not there. In imposing her own constellations on the night sky, Hammond plays with one such human projection: astrology. She calls attention to how astrology influences the way believers see themselves and their experiences. In making her own constellations based on images she uses repeatedly in her artwork, Hammond shows how her signs and symbols fill her mental skies, reflecting and influencing her life and who she is.

Transform. *Change or morph something into something else.* Ellen Jewett transforms or morphs animals into plants to explore the interrelationship between the two. With this transformation, the original creature becomes even grander and more compelling than it would be if it were depicted realistically. In *The White Stag* (2014; see Figure 7.7), Jewett creates a white stag in mid-transformation, still an animal but

FIGURE 7.8. Thomas Dambo, *Future Forest* (2018)

becoming ever more plantlike. Morphing is a common strategy in animation or computer-enhanced live action films, where characters morph into other beings and the step-by-step process of transformation evolves before the viewer's eyes.

In a similar vein, Thomas Dambo transforms garbage into art to create installations that generate consciousness of environmental issues and build community. For example, in the Chapultepec Botanical Garden in Mexico City, Dambo collaborated with trash collectors (*penpenadores*), their children, 700 students, and 100 volunteers to create the *Future Forest* (2018; see Figure 7.8), a maze of plants and animals constructed out of plastic forms and other discarded materials. The result was a playful, colorful, and intricate wonderland that contrasted with the natural environment surrounding it. This is an example of art transforming many things: a park into a wonderland, trash into art, disparate groups into a collaborative community, and community members into artists.

Juxtapose. *Place contrasting images or objects in proximity to each other.* Juxtaposition is a popular strategy for making cultural commentary. Justin Lee, a Singapore artist of Chinese descent, uses this strategy repeatedly in his clever artwork. In *Warrior* (ND; refer to Figure 2.3), Lee plays with the terra-cotta warriors of Xian, China. The terra-cotta warriors (209 BCE) protected the tomb of Qin Shi Huang, the first emperor of China. As remnants of the glory days of Chinese empirical rule, today the warriors are symbols of Chinese culture and represent its longevity and power. Lee juxtaposes these warrior figures with modern-day high-tech paraphernalia that allow people today to tune out of the world around them and tune in to commercial pop culture and entertainment. In this juxtaposition of old icons with new icons, Lee shows us how complex ideas—such as the monumental changes in Chinese culture since the rise of globalization, the pervasiveness and power of global popular culture, the widespread addiction to technological "toys," and the isolation of the individual—can be expressed in a simple juxtaposition of meaningful icons.

Apply a Metaphor. *Cast one thing as another.* Here are two examples of how to approach and use meta-

FIGURE 7.9. Robert Arneson, *Portrait of the Artist as a Clever Old Dog* (1981)

phor. The first approach—image as metaphor—is represented by a self-portrait of Robert Arneson, *Portrait of the Artist as a Clever Old Dog* (1981; see Figure 7.9). In this ceramic sculpture, the artist does not portray himself in a strictly realistic way, but instead presents himself as a wizened old dog surrounded by a dish of unappetizing food and an array of colorful piles of dog droppings. Although the viewer can read this image in multiple ways, it appears that the artist is expressing his whimsical yet melancholy thoughts about his art, his life, and his personality.

Maria Lai's *Bread Encyclopedia* (2008; see Figure 7.10) engages metaphor in a different way. Lai is a book artist whose books are often made of fabric and thread. In the series shown here, however, Lai's book covers are made of flatbread. In using an unusual but meaningful material such as bread for a book cover, Lai surprises the viewer. The work is clever, but why? It is clever because it connects bread to books. In doing so, it taps into the meaning of bread and connects it to the

FIGURE 7.10. Maria Lai, *Bread Encyclopedia* (2008)

FIGURE 7.11. Adam Dant, *Copenhagen* (2018). From *Living Maps: An Atlas of Cities Personified* (Dant, 2018)

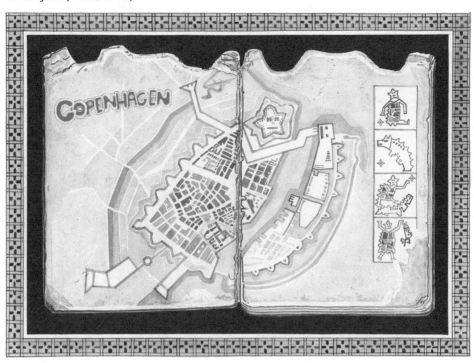

meaning of books. The material (bread) is metaphorical, and it pushes us to see books in a deeper and different way. The artwork is open to interpretation, but the bread metaphor implies that books, in this case encyclopedias, are basic nourishment and essential to life.

Map. *Arrange ideas and imagery in graphic form.* Contemporary artists often make maps (use cartography) to visualize ideas. For example, Lordy Rodriguez makes colorful maps in which real places are rearranged and borders are reconfigured to show how a sense of place is subjective and borders are artificial lines of demarcation. Grayson Perry uses maps to illustrate his life and inner world. Adam Dant (2018) has another approach to mapping. He maps real cities to visualize their history and culture. In his *Living Maps: An Atlas of Cities Personified* (2018), Dant goes a step further in using the creative strategies of metaphor and personification. He illustrates what iconic cities represent. Figure 7.11 is his map of Copenhagen, the city of fairy tales.

In *Survival* (2010; see Figure 7.12), Simon Evans (a husband and wife team of artists) illustrates their thoughts on what it takes to survive. This map differs from the maps discussed previously because it is not an adaptation of a geographical map but instead is a concept map, an abstract graphic representation of relationships. The Evanses are known for conveying personal ideas, experiences, and fantasies through maps and charts—formats taken from the sciences and mathematics. Their diagrammatic depictions highlight the aesthetic qualities of these information formats while they embrace the irony of using them to express subjective ideas. In *Survival,* the Evanses take this a step further; they use the concept map to visualize their thinking. Here art goes beyond picturing concepts to visualizing how those concepts are conceived.

Layer. *Superimpose one image onto another.* Tenmyouya Hisashi's *Adidas Superstar 2003 Version* (see Figure 7.13) is a running shoe fit for a shogun, or at least a samurai. In this elaborate shoe, Hisashi uses the creative strategy of layering—superimposing symbols of ancient samurai culture onto contemporary high-tech sports shoes. In doing so, he fuses an epic warrior culture of old Japan with a contemporary icon of masculinity, competition, and the physical prowess

FIGURE 7.12. Simon Evans, *Survival* (2010)

Figure 7.12 content (labels):

IN LIFE YOU MUST FIGHT AND ACT LIKE YOU KNOW WHATS GOING ON

HUNGER FOR TRANSCENDENCE

HUNGER FOR TRANSCENDENCE

SUCK THE TOTEM OF THE NEAREST GIANT

DO PRESS UPS IN THE CELLAR AT WORK

THE REASON WHY ANYTHING HAPPENS

SPIRIT OF IMPROVEMENT DOING LAPS

PRAYING

NAVIGATE EXISTING SYSTEMS

HAVING THE LUXURY OF FEELINGS

PHYSICAL EXERCISE

LUCK

AVOID FRIENDSHIPS AND WEDDINGS WITH VAMPIRES AND FUCK UPS

MONEY

BE POLITE SO THEY DONT EAT YOU

SURVIVAL

SHELTER

FANTASY GENRE

FOOD AND DRINK

TASTE IS THE ILLUSION OF CLASS

THE T-SHIRT WE FOUGHT CANCER IN

IRONIC T-SHIRTS

EGG

FEEDING OFF A GENERAL FEEDING

DISTINGUISH YOURSELF IN YOUR SUBCULTURE

THE BLURED LINE OF ART AND DESIGN

EXTREMELY SEXUAL SHAPE

AVOID OBVIOUS SOURCES OF ILLNESS

ART RENDERING

GO TO THE EDGE OF THE WORLD AND JOIN A SUBCULTURE

BALANCE

BODIES

PEOPLE

PLUG SCREAMING HOLE

MAKE YOUR TOOLS REALLY SHARP

DIE AND SUCCEED

FIGURE 7.13. Tenmyouya Hisashi, *Adidas Superstar 2003 Version*

associated with athletics. Here the metaphors of both shoe and samurai connect to convey these cultural concepts, but the shoe also speaks of the elaborate rituals and design that surround articles of clothing, particularly those that symbolize identity, glory, and prowess.

In his *High Falutin'* (1990; see Figure 7.14), David Hammons also layers two cultural icons, a basketball hoop and a crystal chandelier, to make a social statement. The two objects in this subtle pairing are rich in cultural meaning: the basketball hoop as the center of young Black male urban life, and the chandelier (represented in the added decorations and lights) as an embodiment of wealth and status. In *High Falutin'*, these icons combine to represent the aspirations of young African American men who see sports as a ladder to success. The basketball hoop becomes an icon of hope and dreams, respect and accomplishment.

Intervene. *Take action.* When artists intervene, they go beyond conveying ideas or making statements to take action to contribute to the world or solve a problem. Thomas Dambo, the artist behind the *Future Forest* (refer to Figure 7.8) intervenes in his use of recycled materials and his many community-based projects. Dambo is also known for intervening to help urban wildlife. One example is his artwork for homeless birds, *Bird House Mural* (2012; see Figure 7.15), a tree of recycled wood hung with birdhouses.

Closing Thoughts on Creative Strategies

The strategies described here are limited to creative strategies that work best for children and adolescents. A more complete list is presented in the accompanying Keys to Understanding feature. No list could ever be complete. There are plenty of strategies yet to be invented. Young learners are good at that. Once students or their teacher create a new creative strategy, they should give it a name and try it again.

STRATEGIES FOR THINKING, INQUIRY, AND LEARNING

How can creative strategies be used to learn? Creative strategies prompt learning in a variety of ways. For example, when we *juxtapose* two contrasting ideas, images, or things, we can discern their differences and their similarities. We learn about them by seeing them in relationship to each other. When we *elaborate* on something, we embellish it with details. We learn more about it by explaining or expanding on it. When we apply a *metaphor* to something, we see it in light of something else; this allows us to understand the subject more fully and to see it from a new angle.

Metaphor is a tool and a process for thinking that directly relates to Perkins's (1988) web of understanding (see Chapter 2). In a metaphor, the subject being "metaphored" takes on the associations of the metaphor being applied to it (Black, 1981; Orotony, 1993). To realize the learning about a subject that comes

FIGURE 7.14. David Hammons, *High Falutin'* (1990)

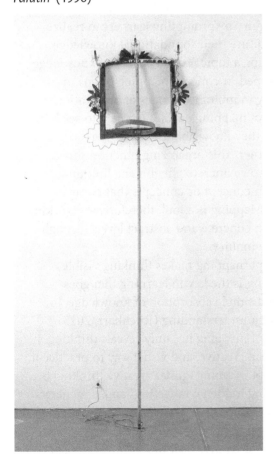

FIGURE 7.15. Thomas Dambo, *Bird House Mural* (2012)

KEYS TO UNDERSTANDING

Creative Strategies from Contemporary Art

- *Change Scale:* Make an object larger or smaller relative to other things
- *Hybridize:* Join parts of different things
- *Personify:* Cast animals or inanimate objects as human
- *Extend:* Take ideas to logical or absurd conclusions
- *Elaborate:* Go into more detail; add details; accumulate connections
- *Project:* Imagine or envision what is not there or speculate on what could happen next
- *Transform:* Morph or change something into something else
- *Employ Metaphor:* Cast one thing as another
- *Use Metaphorical Materials:* Use materials that have meaning in themselves
- *Use Unusual Materials:* Construct an object out of surprising materials and/or components
- *Map:* Arrange and present ideas and concepts in graphic configurations
- *Categorize or Re-categorize:* Place something in its common category, a new category, or multiple categories
- *Juxtapose:* Place contrasting images or objects in proximity to each other
- *Layer:* Superimpose an image onto another image or form
- *Intervene:* Insert an object or image into an environment; take action
- *Distill:* Simplify down to the basic form or idea
- *Reformat:* Use a format from outside art
- *Mimic:* Use the methods of a non-art discipline
- *Embody:* Take on the persona of someone else; act; personify an idea
- *Appropriate:* Use an existing image to draw on its meaning
- *Translate:* Create a form in a different material (often an art material)

through metaphor, we need to grasp its implications or associations. Concept mapping is a great way to do that. Figure 7.16 is my concept map of Robert Arneson's metaphorical self-portrait (refer to Figure 7.9) that shows the many associations that can emerge through concept mapping a metaphor. In mapping this image of *Portrait of the Artist as a Clever Old Dog*, a viewer becomes aware of the attributes associated with "dog," "art," "food," and "age"—what Arneson may have had in mind when he saw himself as a mischievous aging puppy. Figure 7.17 is a 5th-grader's version of a concept map of the same artwork. It shows the first steps of investigation: observation and commentary.

From these examples, one can see that concept mapping is a creative strategy with potential for prompting thinking and learning from an artwork. Concept maps have many applications. Most often, they are used for collaborative idea generation. In creative inquiry, however, concept mapping goes beyond idea generation. It does this in six ways:

- Concept mapping provides a broad foundation for inquiry by prompting learners to realize and capture their foundational knowledge regarding a topic. The rich store of knowledge developed in concept mapping opens up inquiry to multiple avenues of exploration.
- Concept mapping enables learners to see how things they know about a topic are related to each other. This organizing function shows them how concrete phenomena link up to reveal a concept or concepts that connect them. Mapping is a tool, therefore, for working on both concrete and abstract levels throughout the inquiry.
- Concept mapping makes thinking visible. Thinking is the key to learning that goes beyond simple absorption of knowledge, to building understanding (Ritchhart, 2015). Concept mapping not only reveals thinking, it is a clear, creative, and visual way to practice it.
- Concept mapping ignites creative thinking by revealing hidden connections and/or generating new connections. Here concept mapping builds on its spontaneous, open-ended, and unfiltered nature. It allows learners/mappers

FIGURE 7.16. Concept Map of Robert Arneson's *Portrait of the Artist as a Clever Old Dog*

FIGURE 7.17. Dinah Cooper, Concept Map of Robert Arneson's *Portrait of the Artist as a Clever Old Dog*

to reveal and construct fresh, seemingly non-sensical connections that broaden or transform their understanding. Figure 7.18 shows a concept map by Summer, a 2nd-grader at the Creative Arts Charter School in San Francisco. With this map, she began her inquiry into plants and what they do for us in a project that is discussed in the next section on the research workbook.

- Concept maps can be collaborative and capture what learners know or think about a topic of mutual interest or concern. These maps help learners share ideas and learn from each other. Figure 7.19 is a collage mural by students in Meredith Charpentier's 5th-grade class at Grattan Elementary School in San Francisco in which class members illustrated and organized their knowledge and ideas about what causes environmental and social problems (greed, represented by a dollar bill). Notice that this map uses visual imagery and symbols instead of words. On the margin are the questions that prompted their inquiry.

- Concept maps can also reveal and record the accumulation of knowledge and ideas over time. This could entail learners making initial maps of what they know and think about topics while adding more information and ideas to the maps as they accumulate. Creating a series

of individual maps that build upon each other is another way to record and push learners' process. In the next section on the research workbook, Kyle's intricate maps show how his knowledge and ideas expanded and progressed as he explored his topic and followed various topics related to it.

THE RESEARCH WORKBOOK

The research workbook is an effective tool for student learning through creative inquiry, as well as for curriculum integration. These books are quite different from the sketchbooks commonly associated with art. More like scientific field study books, research workbooks focus on investigation and cover all that goes into an inquiry. Since their origin is in the natural and social sciences, research workbooks are instances of integration through method and form. Although research workbooks may follow a model from the

FIGURE 7.18. Summer Christensen, Concept Map of the Notion of Plant

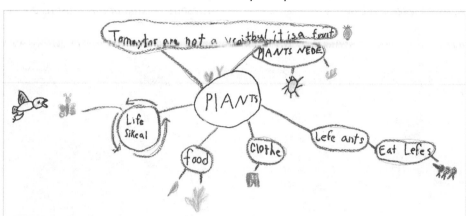

sciences and serve as background for works of art, they are artworks in themselves. They represent an "interstitial" or hybrid form of art, one that emerges when art meets learning and uses a form from the sciences to do it.

Benefits of the Research Workbook

The value of having students create research workbooks has many dimensions, as explored below:

- Research workbooks are excellent vehicles for integration because each book chronicles how a learner follows a trail and connects the topic or topics of his or her inquiry to a variety of information and ideas from the academic domains.
- Research workbooks are the most generative and effective way to tie a creative art-based investigation together. The book is where learners store and arrange their resource mate-

FIGURE 7.19. *How Are All Our Issues Connected?*

rials, map connections to their topic(s), illustrate their ideas, record their thoughts, make their plans, and experiment with materials and ideas while they chronicle their process.

- Research workbooks foster creativity. Since they are constructed over time, students can make connections they might not otherwise make. They can revisit ideas and combine them with subsequent ideas to create something new.
- Research workbooks are multimodal works of scholarship. In them, visual images complement discursive, creative, and reflective writing to reveal, build, and deepen learners' understandings of topics.
- Research workbooks make the *process* of learning about topics both visible and tangible. As learners add to their books, they observe themselves learning about a topic, particularly since the book includes all steps in their investigation, thinking, and interpretation of the subject. Because research workbooks are an extended chronicle of their learning, students can see how their learning progresses over time. The workbooks enable learners to go back, revisit, add to, and revise things, and to rework ideas and imagery in different, more informed ways. The workbooks give learners the opportunity to teach themselves—to learn from their own work. Revisiting and revising are critical to learning from one's art and also to refining it. While younger learners can revise their work and learn from it, making multiple revisions is best suited to more mature learners.
- Research workbooks are personal. When learners create these books, they become deeply engaged with ideas and information and they write their own books. Young people often become attached to their books and find great satisfaction in creating and owning them. Learners also develop a sense of agency because the books are tangible reminders that they are the authors of their own learning. It is important for learners to remember that, however personal a research workbook is, it is also meant to be read by others and to be critiqued by peers and teacher alike.

- Research workbooks are excellent vehicles for assessment, a final benefit that belongs to the teacher. They can reveal what and how a young person learned in the most detailed and visible ways. Furthermore, they give teachers a clearer vision of how their courses are going and how their teaching is working. Beyond this, because the workbooks are creative and aesthetic artworks, they can be a joy to look at, read, and assess. This makes assessment easier and more meaningful, and it keeps teachers more closely in touch with their students.

For more on research workbooks and their origins, take a look at the International Baccalaureate Program, where research workbooks are the backbone of art-based inquiry (see www.ibo.org and www.artasresearch.org).

Two Models of the Research Workbook

There are two basic models of the research workbook, as described below.

Model One: Curriculum-Based Inquiry. The first model works with curriculum, art or otherwise, that is a sequence of teacher-initiated projects or lessons along a curriculum trail. The research workbook, in this context, is a learner's chronicle of their learning over the course of a curriculum. The topic investigated is the throughline of the curriculum (see Teaching for Understanding in Chapter 8). The advantage of this model is that it is adaptable to existing curriculum and can enhance and reorient it. Couching projects within the context of an extended inquiry can change a fragmented sequence of lessons or projects into an extended art-based inquiry, and using a research workbook can enable learners to see the thread, the throughline, that links the projects along the trail To orient a curriculum toward inquiry, teachers must rethink and revise their curriculum to stress inquiry with its open-ended questions, investigation, and personal interpretation. They must also clarify, strengthen, and stress the connections among the projects or lessons.

This first model of the research workbook introduces learners to the inquiry approach to learning and helps them to build and practice skills they can use in further, more independent inquiry. It is adaptable to all grade levels (1–12), and it is highly recommended for elementary and early middle school.

Starting early and building the skills and dispositions inherent in inquiry at an early age is helpful. It is also important to build these skills slowly and methodically. In other words, the project-by-project model of the research workbook is where learners can begin. Early adventures into creative inquiry and research workbooks should be simple, amply structured, and highly scaffolded.

Figures 7.20 through 7.24 are examples of artwork in research workbooks from Grace Wilson and Katie Brinkley's 2nd-grade classes at the Creative Arts Charter School in San Francisco. These illustrations were created by Lina and Lucy during their classes' month-long inquiry into plants. In the project, the 2nd-graders investigated plants, conducted plant experiments, did observational drawings, and designed a hybrid plant with superpowers to treat a problem in their community. A version of this project is described in detail in Chapter 9.

Model Two: Independent Research. When learners become attuned to and skilled in the kinds of thinking and art making involved in creative inquiry, they are ready to do more independent investigations. This is where the second model of the research workbook comes in. In the second model, learners use their research workbooks to record and construct their own personal investigations into topics of interest to them. Although these books chronicle independent research and are shaped by personal inquiry more than by teacher-initiated activities, they still require structure and scaffolding. This is especially true for learning artists who are not accustomed to designing their own "curriculum" or independently blazing their own trail (see Marshall & D'Adamo [2018] for more about this).

FIGURE 7.20. Lucy Shaw, Concept Map of a Plant from Her Research Workbook

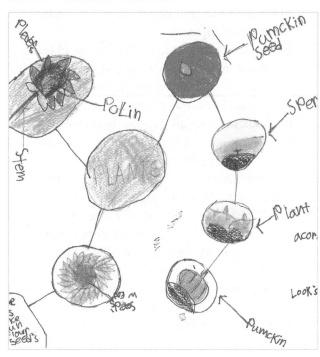

FIGURE 7.21. Lucy Shaw, Scientific Drawings from Her Research Workbook

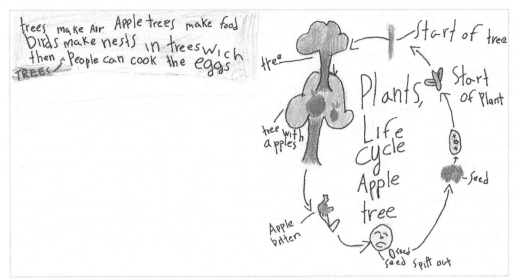

FIGURE 7.22.
Lina Boyko, Map of the Life Cycle of a Plant from Her Research Workbook

trees make Air Apple trees make food
birds make nests in trees wich
then ↑ People can cook the eggs
TREES

tree

tree with apples

Plants, Life Cycle Apple tree

Apple bitten

Seed seed spitt out

Start of tree

Start of Plant

seed

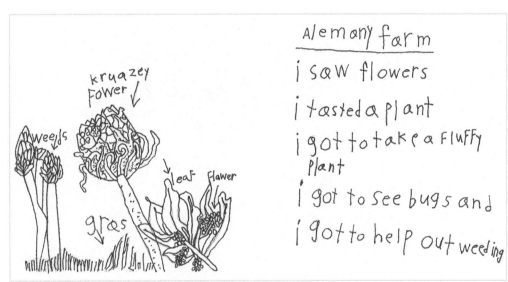

FIGURE 7.23.
Lucy Shaw, Reflections from Her Research Workbook

kruazey Fower

weeds

leaf Flawer

gras

Alemany farm
i saw flowers
i tasted a plant
i got to take a Fluffy Plant
i got to see bugs and
i got to help out weeding

FIGURE 7.24.
Lucy Shaw, Drawing of a Superpower Plant from Her Research Workbook

BACK TO THE ROOTS

RDEN-IN-A can

rw organic
nts right
of this coun

Rose

Gerber-Daisy

Gerber-Rose

It's Superpower is...
To Make Kindeniss!
So the earth can have Kindeniss!

Examples of independent inquiry scaffolding come to us from Liz McAvoy's middle school art classes at Francisco Middle School in San Francisco. Figures 7.25 to 7.27 are from two research workbooks, which illustrate two activities Ms. McAvoy used for introducing the notion of art-based inquiry. These drawings illustrate steps in the introductory scaffolding activities. The first activity entailed drawing, interviewing, and concept mapping a personal object (see Figure 7.25).

The second activity involved learners using the same strategies to investigate their shoes (Figure 7.26) and then design a new shoe (Figure 7.27). This second activity allowed students to practice the skills they had learned in the prior activity while it introduced imagination and invention into the inquiry.

Creating a new shoe was not the only instance of creativity in these activities, however. Both exercises utilized the creative strategies of personification and projection when the students interviewed their objects and shoes. The list of questions students generated for their interviews shows how imaginative—and hilarious—this activity can become.

After these two scaffolding activities, the students began their searches for topics to research. Figures 7.28 and 7.29 reflect the first steps in Kyle's individual

FIGURE 7.25. Sarah Knight-Weiss, Map of Her Key Chain

FIGURE 7.26. Kyle Chau, Concept Map of His Shoe

research. Figure 7.28 shows Kyle surveying a myriad of the topics related to his central theme: the modern military. Figure 7.29 includes Kyle's subsequent maps. These maps show further research and how Kyle revisited and added to his maps as he acquired information

and developed ideas for the artworks and inquiry that followed.

There are advantages to doing independent art-based inquiry in middle school art classes. First, unlike high school students, middle school students often do not have fixed ways of thinking about art; they are more likely to embrace art as a way of investigation rather than as a set of skills, as the production of expressive aesthetic products, or as a domain with rules of right and wrong.

Second, middle school students are, for the most part, developmentally ready to tackle this challenge. Teachers, however, must provide this age-group with clear guidelines and use simple, focused scaffolding activities that bring students along. They also must provide resources, recommendations for topics and ideas for research, suggestions for directions a research topic might take, and examples of research-based art. I recommend that each individual inquiry start with a "small idea," or specific concrete topic, and then, as the research progresses, connect that topic to Big Ideas

FIGURES 7.27. Sarah Knight-Weiss, Shoe Designs from Her Research Workbook

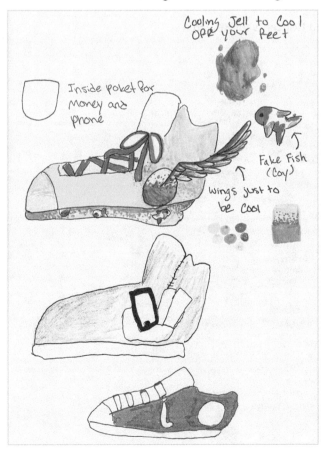

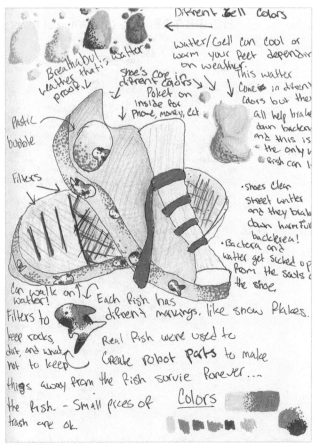

KEYS TO UNDERSTANDING

Some Questions for Interviewing Shoes from Ms. McAvoy's Middle School Art Class

- What food do you like?
- Do you like the smell of my foot?
- How do you feel every day being suffocated by a foot?
- Do you believe in magic?
- Where are you from?
- Can you talk?
- Can you stop talking? *You're freaking me out.*
- Do you have genders? *I will marry a shoe.*
- Are your different brands different races?
- Why did your designer make you look like that? *He/she/they did a bad job.*
- Can shoes get plastic surgery?
- How do you live, normally? (When you're not on a foot)
- Do you like K-Pop?
- Do you like getting tied hard?
- What is attractive for a shoe?

- How do you feel when you're just bought and you fall in a pool with mud?
- Do you get mad when somebody steps on you?
- Do you ever need to take a bath?
- How do you feel when you get flung?
- Do you like being tied over power cords?
- Do you watch anime?
- If you have a mouth, how can you eat? (You have a tongue, but where's your mouth?)
- Did you kill your previous owner?
- How many languages can you speak, and what languages can you speak?
- What happens if you step on dog poo?
- Are horseshoes actually horses for you guys?
- Is your best friend a sock?
- What are your opinions on closets?
- Do you feel sad when your owner throws you away?
- Do you sleep?

FIGURE 7.28. Kyle Chau, Map of Ideas and Concepts for Research

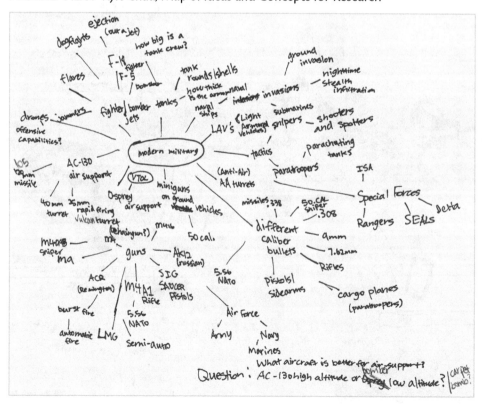

FIGURE 7.29. Kyle Chau, Venn Diagram and Illustration of Ideas for Research

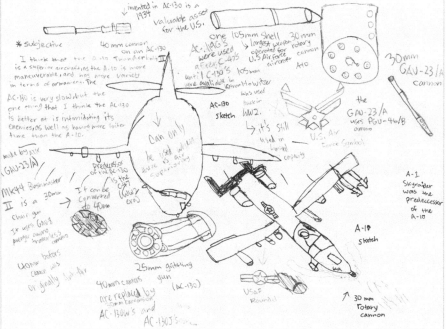

and concepts. It is far easier to start small as long as the topic is generative (has potential for leading to significant ideas and to connections that are expansive and creative). That is why Liz McAvoy's class started with concrete objects like shoes and key chains. These objects harbor many personal and cultural associations and offer multiple opportunities for exploring them and their meaning.

It is also helpful for students to work together and help each other through class collaborations, such as group brainstorming and idea sharing, creative group activities separate from their individual research, and friendly small-group critiques (Marshall & D'Adamo, 2018).

Third, research workbooks enable middle school students to draw connections among the various subjects they study in their academic classes. As they follow a topic, they explore it through the lens of different disciplines. They can blend what they are learning in their academic classes into the art-based inquiry. In this model of curriculum integration, the student artist-researcher is the "integrator," the one who finds the disciplinary connections around a specific topic or topics.

For detailed ideas for scaffolding independent inquiry in middle school and high school, look at examples of inquiry-based art and pedagogy at www.artasresearch.org, a website dedicated to art-based research that features curriculum and student work from Kimberley D'Adamo's classes at Berkeley High School.

THE FOREGOING discussion about the intersection of creativity and learning and the tools teachers can use to foster both leads now to frameworks teachers can utilize to systematically think through, develop, and organize curriculum in which creative art making and learning strategies can be applied.

8

Frameworks and Strategies for Curriculum and Pedagogy

HOW DO educators put inquiry-based art integration into practice? What tools and strategies can they use? This chapter tackles those questions with explanations of Harvard University's Project Zero (PZ) frameworks and how they can be used to

- Provide a rich environment for thinking and learning
- Impose smart, durable, and flexible open structures that give learners something to hang on to, bounce off of, and play within
- Supply learning "ladders" or sets of learning experiences that help students to achieve complex and meaningful understandings of a topic while they develop into independent, highly motivated learners
- Create an environment in which students learn from and teach each other while they learn from themselves

Although the PZ frameworks were originally intended for building understanding of academic content, many PZ ideas either come from the arts (ongoing assessment in the form of portfolios), are inherent in making art ("performances of understanding" or processes that both build and demonstrate understanding simultaneously), or use visual imagery to convey ideas. It makes sense that these frameworks, which owe so much to hands-on, minds-on art practice, bring their added wisdom, vocabulary, and structure to the model of art-based inquiry.

UTILIZING THE PROJECT ZERO FRAMEWORKS

Project Zero provides ideas—through a series of frameworks—for delivering three fundamentals of creative inquiry: conducive environment, effective guidance, and strong but flexible structure.

Regarding environment, Project Zero's Ron Ritchhart (2015) makes a strong case for transforming classrooms into *cultures of thinking*—environments that emphasize thinking, and actively nurture and support it. The Studio Thinking Framework (Hetland et al., 2013) emphasizes the studio nature of a creative inquiry-based classroom. In regard to structure, Teaching for Understanding (TfU) (Blythe & Perkins, 1998; Wiske, 1998) provides a framework for curriculum design that helps teachers and learners be more intentional and thoughtful. As to guidance, TfU and Making Thinking Visible (MTV) (Ritchhart, Church, & Morrison, 2011) provide scaffolding strategies and protocols that promote thinking. Lastly, Making Learning Visible (MLV) (Krechevsky et al., 2013) offers ideas for documentation that promote learning and metacognition. These four frameworks, which I discuss in this chapter, work together to build the culture of thinking that Ritchhart (2015) envisions and the structure and scaffolding that support creative inquiry.

Making Thinking Visible

Making Thinking Visible explicitly emphasizes thinking as the key to meaningful learning. To build understanding, learners must think. This contrasts with the conventional notion that students must learn content before they can think about it. Learning through thinking has an added benefit. When learners think to learn, they also learn to think. Toward these ends, Making Thinking Visible offers specific protocols for prompting thought and developing thinking skills (see Ritchhart et al., 2011). It should be noted that by the term "visible," MTV means learning is articulated and made accessible, which does not always entail visual documentation or representation.

Making Learning Visible

Making Learning Visible provides a broad vision of learning. It asserts that learning is purposeful, social, emotional, representational, and empowering. All five of these traits are highlighted in Making Learning Visible's concept of education and are realized through MLV's primary tool: the learning wall—a mural-like map of ideas, thinking, creation, and reflection created by learners as they progress through their inquiry (refer to Figure 1.6).

The purpose of a learning wall (and MLV) is to showcase thinking and learning over time. The wall presents a timeline of learning that enables learners to see how learning progresses in ways that are both linear and nonlinear. It allows them to see what prompts, supports, extends, and expands their learning as it evolves, thus helping learners to become more metacognitive.

Furthermore, a learning wall represents what is learned and how it is learned in visual imagery and verbal explanations, stories, and descriptions. When students convey their ideas and knowledge through visual imagery and writing, they learn. When they view and revisit their depictions on the wall, they learn. A wall, therefore, teaches through representing and reflecting on what is portrayed. This highlights the representational nature of learning.

An important social aspect of learning walls is that they are collaborative works in which students learn from each other as they learn and create together. Students derive an emotional benefit from a learning wall in that they become aware of how they learn, and this brings satisfaction and the motivation to do more.

Motivation is further raised when a learning wall reveals the purposefulness of learning. Students learn when they know there's a reason for it. A learning wall can help them see that reason. All in all, Making Learning Visible uses images and maps as learning tools that help learners become socially engaged, intentional, metacognitive, and enthusiastic learners (Krechevsky et al., 2013).

The Studio Thinking Framework: Studio Habits of Mind

The Studio Thinking Framework is useful to the creative inquiry-based approach because it draws attention toward how and what students learn in an art classroom.

Art classrooms are studios; they are places where learners think and learn as they create art. In observing art classes, Lois Hetland and her colleagues (Hetland et al., 2013; Hogan, Hetland, Jacquith, & Winner, 2018) identified eight Studio Habits of Mind (SHoM) that learners perform in an art class:

- Observe
- Envision
- Express
- Reflect
- Stretch and explore
- Engage and persist
- Understand the art world
- Develop craft

Designating these "habits" has important benefits. First, it shifts the focus away from the *products* of art making and toward the *process* of art making. Second, it draws attention to the distinctive behaviors inherent in studio-based learning. These are behaviors that require thinking and promote understanding. Third, the Studio Thinking Framework gives explicit names to these behaviors. In so doing, it makes them easy to spot and, therefore, more easily practiced and honed. With them, students and teachers have a vocabulary they can use to communicate about process and learning outcomes. When they reflect on their work, students have words they can use to articulate what they did.

An emphasis on studio habits stands in stark contrast to more product-centered approaches to art education, where formal and technical issues are the focal points of reflection and critique. Indeed, the SHoM help to break the stifling tradition of valuing exclusively artistic skills and beautiful or expressive artworks. In a studio thinking classroom, everyone can excel at one or more habits. Furthermore, two of the habits—"stretch and explore" and "engage and persist"—promote risk taking, learning from mistakes, and venturing into unknown territory. These habits, in particular, are crucial to creativity and creative inquiry-based learning. That is why the Studio Thinking Framework promotes creative inquiry and also provides criteria for assessment of student performances in the creative inquiry mode.

Finally, the studio habits delineate behaviors that are not exclusive to the art class. Studios are any place where learning occurs through inquiry. Science labs where students explore and experiment are the most obvious example of this kind of environment, but any classroom or laboratory where open-ended inquiry and student-centered learning takes place is home to the studio habits. Thus the habits are cross-disciplinary. On top of that, they connect classroom learning to the "real" work of the disciplines by reflecting what happens in professional research environments. They are, therefore, another strand of curriculum integration.

Teaching for Understanding Framework

Teaching for Understanding (TfU) rests on four key questions:

- What topics are worth understanding?
- What about these topics must learners understand?
- How can teachers foster understanding?
- How can teachers know what students understand?

Teaching for Understanding aligns with creative art-based inquiry because it asks those questions and provides a strong, flexible structure on which to explore them. Furthermore, TfU focuses learners' and teachers' attention on what matters. It requires all learning activities to connect to significant overarching *generative themes* and related goals. In this way, it helps teachers be more intentional in their curriculum and pedagogy. It also leads teachers to develop curriculum that explores themes of consequence to both learners and teachers, and to think through and organize their lessons according to their goals in investigating those themes. TfU also contributes a common vocabulary for educators to use in their teaching and, when used schoolwide, a language for collaborating with their peers.

While Teaching for Understanding helps teachers, it also benefits learners because TfU provides learners with a vocabulary to articulate and communicate their thinking and learning. It also makes the goals of the curriculum and their relationship to overarching themes and other significant ideas explicit. In doing so, it makes curriculum transparent and purposeful for students; it makes learning expectations clear and the pedagogy that supports them understandable. If the goals are worth reaching and make sense, students will "buy in"; they will be motivated to commit to the goals. They will also come to appreciate the teacher, the curriculum, and its supporting pedagogy. Transparency in curriculum also helps students become far more aware of their learning and how it is fostered. With this metacognitive understanding of the curriculum, learners are ready to go beyond simply buying in, to collaborating with the teacher to adapt and grow the curriculum to make it more effective and relevant to them (Marshall & D'Adamo, 2018).

The following are the basic tenets of the Teaching for Understanding Framework.

Generative Themes. Broad topics (also referred to as Big Ideas), generative themes are central to the domain or discipline. They are accessible and interesting to students, interesting to the teacher, and linked to students' experiences and important across the disciplines.

Throughlines. Complex themes that can be explored in many ways, throughlines provide the conceptual thread that connects all the learning experiences in the curriculum and, therefore, bring continuity to a curriculum or inquiry trail.

Understanding Goals. Specific ideas, concepts, and thinking students will come to understand through participating in a particular lesson, a series of lessons, or a project, understanding goals fit with the throughline. Also, they pertain to significant issues and concepts, not to technical skills or discipline-specific "principles." In art, understanding goals, therefore, are about grasping concepts and making meaning, and not about formal concerns or crafts-manship. Those goals are procedural in nature and can be listed in a separate category as process goals.

Generative Questions. A Teaching for Under-standing lesson begins with a generative question or two. Generative questions are linked to the through-line and understanding goals of the lesson or project. These questions are research questions that help learn-ers focus on the important facets of a theme. Since they are questions and not answers, these questions initiate inquiry. To be generative, they must be open-ended and thought provoking and must have no easy yes or no answers. Generative questions probe signifi-cant concepts and ideas of importance to the learner, the discipline(s), and the world outside school. Gen-erative questions are conceptual and not about skills, craft, formal qualities, or technique.

Performances of Understanding. The learning activities in a lesson, "performances of understand-ing" may seem like an arcane term for activities, but there is a reason for this. TfU and other PZ frame-works are grounded in the Performance Theory of Understanding (Perkins, 1988)—the notion that learning experiences should be ways learners build understanding and also demonstrate understanding at the same time. As hands-on, minds-on endeavors, performances are not mere exercises but are activities that spur and require thinking. These performances directly connect to the understanding goals.

Guiding Questions. Guiding questions are far more focused and concrete than generative questions. They are specific to each inquiry. Their role is to help learners enter into an inquiry and then to steer them

toward more complex abstract thinking and signifi-cant Big Ideas. Think of guiding questions as a ladder of questions. On the bottom rung are simple, concrete questions learners can answer easily because they directly connect to them. The questions become more and more thought provoking and open-ended as they progress up the ladder. Because these questions tap into learners' knowledge or experience in very specific and tangible ways, they help learners take what they know from their lives or from school, expand upon it, connect it to Big Ideas or concepts, and transform it into artworks. Guiding questions also help learners build a variety of tangible ideas on which to base their artwork.

Reflection. Reflection activities are performances of understanding in which learners observe, analyze, and synthesize what they have learned and how they have learned it. They are performances of under-standing because learners do them to learn as well as to demonstrate their understanding. As Dewey (1902) argued, learning occurs not in just doing something, but in doing it and then reflecting on the experi-ence. Reflection is where the learning surfaces and is realized.

Reflection Questions. Reflection questions drive the reflection and make it probing and meaningful. With these questions, the learners' attention is drawn back to the understanding goals. Attention is also directed toward the process learners went through to reach an understanding. This includes the thinking they did, the decisions they made, the connections they constructed, and the knowledge they employed. Reflection questions, therefore, go beyond simple questions such as Do you like what you made? What do you like about it? How would you change it?

Ongoing Assessment. Teaching for Understand-ing places a great deal of emphasis on ongoing assess-ment as opposed to stand-alone, one-time summative assessment. Here, assessment becomes a crucial part of the scaffolding in the lesson/project and, therefore, is of benefit to the learning process. Ongoing assessment supports students in their learning; it helps students learn and progress throughout the inquiry. This is in stark contrast to summative assessment, which, as a

KEYS TO UNDERSTANDING

Teaching for Understanding Inquiry/Project Plan

- *Project or Lesson Title:* What you call the inquiry or project
- *Overview:* Short statement of what students will do, research, and make
- *Throughline:* The overarching theme that threads through the entire curriculum
- *Generative Theme:* The theme that underlies the series of inquiries or projects in the unit and this specific inquiry/project
- *Understanding Goals:* What you want learners to understand about the generative theme. These goals are conceptual and primarily cross-disciplinary.
- *Skills and Secondary Goals:* Goals that are more discipline-specific and procedural
- *Generative Questions:* Questions you ask to address and penetrate the Big Ideas and reach the understanding goals. These are often the understanding goals in question form.
- *Vocabulary:* Important words in the lesson
- *Materials:* Art materials and instructional materials you will use
- *Equipment:* Tools you use in instruction and in art making
- *Generative Exercises:* Warm-up and scaffolding activities for the inquiry/project
- *Guiding Questions:* More focused questions that help learners enter into an inquiry, help them ground it in specific personal information and "instances," and help them develop ideas. Guiding

questions permeate the whole inquiry/project. However, they most often help to launch one.
- *Performances of Understanding:* Hands-on, minds-on activity or activities learners will do. In art-based inquiry, these activities are often making artworks, including maps, sketches, and/or "finished" pieces.
- *Closure:* Activity or activities that will close the inquiry/project. These activities often "wrap it up." They can be critiques, discussions, exhibitions, performances, games, or more artwork.
- *Reflection Tools and Techniques:* Methods students will use to assess what they have learned and how they learned it. Tools can include protocols (see Ritchhart et al., 2011).
- *Reflection Questions:* Questions you ask to generate reflection and build understanding. These questions tie directly to understanding goals and address the process, particularly the ideas generated and expressed in the artworks and the thinking and learning that took place.
- *Ongoing Assessment:* How you will assess learning throughout the lesson. This can take the form of questionnaires, reflective writings, discussions, interviews, and observation of students at work.
- *Criteria for Assessment:* The criteria you will use in your assessment. The Studio Habits of Mind provide a variety of criteria for assessment. To the SHoM, I recommend adding understanding of the concept as a primary goal/criterion to assess.

---

final isolated judgment on a learner's work or understanding, does not promote learning as much as judge it. Assessment, therefore, is a form of performance of understanding; it builds understanding as it evaluates it. Assessment also connects directly to the understanding goals. This gives the lesson or project cohesion and reinforces why the lesson exists in the first place. When it is ongoing, assessment also becomes more egalitarian, more student driven. It can also enable students and teachers to understand how a learner thinks, learns, and makes meaning over time.

Documentation. Thorough ongoing documentation tracks the learning process and the kinds of thinking and creation that take place in it. Documentation is critical to teachers and students alike because it reveals what students understand and how they came to understand it, which helps learners become metacognitive. Documentation also makes visible the interaction between pedagogy and learning, thus helping teachers assess their curriculum and teaching. Beyond that, documentation can be an advocacy tool: It demonstrates to others the richness and depth of learning that takes place in creative art-based inquiry and learning. Documentation, therefore, is a scaffolding tool for learning, an assessment tool for teachers, and a powerful way to communicate to parents and administrators how vital, rich, and effective creative inquiry is. Documentation is best when it includes descriptions of activities and scaffolding; generative, guiding, and reflection questions; quotes from learners and teachers; photographs of learners exploring and creating; and other visual imagery, such as artworks and concept maps. Documentation can be displayed on learning walls and in research workbooks.

Teaching for Understanding, Creative Inquiry, and Integration

How does Teaching for Understanding promote creative inquiry? How can establishing understanding goals or final outcomes align with the open-ended quality of creative inquiry? How does TfU promote curriculum integration? The answers to these questions are really quite simple.

- Creative inquiry-based learning requires structure, focus, and guidance. Without them, students get lost and learning does not progress (Kirschner, Sweller, & Clark, 2006). TfU and the other Project Zero frameworks provide these necessities.
- Reconciling intentionality (understanding goals or outcomes) with the open-ended, improvisational nature of creative inquiry is easily done when understanding creative inquiry through practicing it is one of the understanding goals.
- TfU aligns with creative inquiry in its emphasis on questions. TfU discourages providing answers and instead promotes asking questions, particularly questions that are thought-provoking and push the inquiry forward.
- In regard to integration, TfU emphasizes addressing themes and topics that are significant and related to the world of students. These themes naturally transcend disciplinary boundaries. A thorough creative investigation into them is inherently integrative.

CREATIVE CURRICULUM DEVELOPMENT: MAKING TRAILS

This section is a guide to developing curriculum for creative art-based inquiry and integration. Here I address the question *How can a teacher develop curriculum that integrates the wisdom and structures of the Project Zero frameworks with creative inquiry?* I begin with the principle that teachers should be the designers of their own curriculum so they can adapt education frameworks and scaffolding models to fit their particular environment and students' needs. Teaching for Understanding provides a general map for a curriculum structure or trail (see Figure 8.1).

Developing a curriculum is not a linear process. I find I bounce back and forth from designing specific projects to mapping out a trail. This is because one project leads to another and, in developing a project, I often come up with more ideas and find new connections. In the discussion that follows, I have divided the process into two parts: (1) developing and mapping a curriculum trail and (2) designing specific projects on the trail.

Before you begin designing lessons and figuring out their sequence, I suggest establishing a throughline—the lens through which all projects and activities are viewed and the thread that unites them. Like research questions, throughlines help us to focus on what is at the core of the work—the central understanding goal or goals. For that reason, a throughline is both specific and universal. An example of a throughline for an art class or a general class is *Artists explore and interpret our interconnected world.* Because a curriculum has so many facets, topics, and goals in it, identifying one throughline may be difficult. I suggest listing all the rationales behind your projects to see where they connect. Try to distill these connections down to one overarching theme. Remember that each lesson or project along the throughline will be an exploration of the theme through a specific topic related to it. After you develop your curriculum and experiment with it, revisit your throughline. It may need adjustment. You may have discovered a better one. It is also all right to have a couple of throughlines. In integrated curriculum, there often are two of them.

FIGURE 8.1. Map of Teaching for Understanding Curriculum

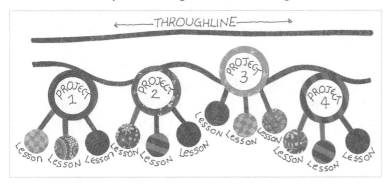

Developing and Mapping a Trail

The steps teachers can follow in planning an integrated project trail are described below.

Step 1: Determine the Big Ideas Behind the Topics on the Trail. In the TfU model, a teacher starts with ascertaining the *Big Ideas* or *Generative Topics* behind the various subject matters to be investigated on the trail and identifies what is important for young people to understand about them. For the sake of clarity, I will use an example that mingles science, social studies, and art: using art-based methods to investigate systems and how things in both nature and the social world function as systems. This trail follows both aspects of the throughline put forth above: the lens of the artist and the interconnectedness of the world.

For determining Big Ideas on the trail, a teacher concept maps all the possibilities for topics and investigations connected to the throughline(s) and understanding goals (see Figure 8.2). In this example, these concepts could be systems in nature and how they work, culture and how we see social groups and social behavior in terms of systems, how our classroom or neighborhoods are systems, and how we can apply the idea of systems to other things through creative writing and art.

Step 2: Map Out a Sequence of Lessons, Activities, and Projects. Once some projects or activities are identified, the next task is to map the curriculum or lay out the sequence of the projects and activities. To facilitate this mapping, it might help to think of the curriculum metaphorically. As mentioned earlier in this book, the metaphor for the curriculum is a trail. The trail metaphor is particularly apt because it implies a linear pathway that has crossroads and branches. Each step on the trail is both a challenge and a pleasure. A trail also can wind its way through a

FIGURE 8.2. Concept Map of a Project Trail Exploring Systems

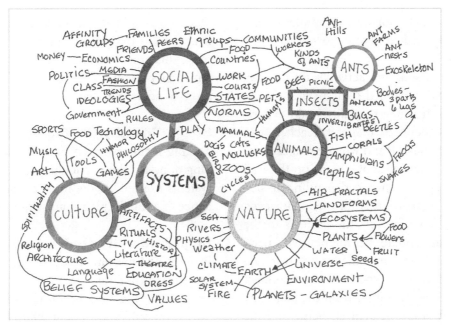

variety of terrains and ecosystems. Although it may have forks in the road or double back on itself, a trail goes somewhere; it is purposeful.

Furthermore, an inquiry trail should have a variety of sign posts, rest spots, and look-out sites. These are the scaffolding activities, lessons, and projects in the inquiry. These lessons should build on one another toward understanding of the Big Ideas. For an example, see Trail #3 in Chapter 9, An Imaginary Island World, where the trail begins with geology and environment and progresses toward social studies and the traits of a civilization.

An important part of mapping a curriculum trail is selecting a portal or entry point onto the trail. Prospective portals can be topics in the academic curriculum, significant ideas and issues from outside school, and other subjects that address the overarching theme of the curriculum and pique learners' interest and curiosity. A portal can be meeting a Big Idea head-on—addressing it right away. This is shown in the 1st-grade project described in Chapter 1, which was launched with the question *What is community?* A portal can also be one facet of the theme that establishes a foundation for subsequent investigations (see Trail #3: An Imaginary Island World, in Chapter 9). There are many ways to start an inquiry, but some are better than others. The bottom line is that portals should be generative. They should open up many possibilities for thought, imagination, invention, and discovery. They should be springboards that launch an investigation and propel it forward. Examples of art-integrated inquiries with different portals are discussed in Chapter 9.

The sequence of lessons and activities on the trail should draw on and expand the inquiry. It should include a variety of learning modalities and experiences. Once the sequence is mapped, teachers can revise the order of projects if and when it makes sense to do so. That is, the sequence of lessons on the trail can be flexible and open to change, depending on students' needs and what works best for them. However, the central thread that connects the projects to the understanding goals should be maintained. Each learning experience must contribute toward reaching the goals. Furthermore, each experience must connect to the other ones. Straying too far from the path may take attention away from the central theme and the

understanding goals. It is also important for teachers to tell students how all the activities, projects, and lessons link together to make a trail toward their goals.

In a curriculum exploring systems, the trail could follow a sequence of lessons and activities such as the following. (This series of projects is inspired by inquiry trails from the Creative Arts Charter School [see community project in Chapter 1] and the ant farm project from Ron Buchanan's kindergarten class at CACS.)

- *Lesson 1:* Study ant bodies as living systems.
- *Lesson 2:* Plant a garden and observe how all the plants, insects (ants and bees), and gardeners (learners) fit into or disrupt the natural order.
- *Lesson 3:* Make and observe an ant farm.
- *Lesson 4:* Make a collage mural of an ant nest (or ant farm) (see Figure 8.3).
- *Lesson 5:* Make a floor plan (map) of the classroom as an ant nest/farm.
- *Lesson 6:* Create and wear ant costumes and act as ants in the ant nest/farm-classroom.
- *Lesson 7:* Illustrate how all the people in your school participate in your school community (system).
- *Lesson 8:* Map the school community as a system like an ant nest/farm.

Designing a Project

Once an integrated project trail has been mapped out, it is time to design the specifics of the projects. To make this process clear, I focus on a lesson in the systems trail presented here: Lesson 5, mapping the classroom as an ant nest/farm.

Step 1: Identify the Big Ideas in the Project. The Big Ideas are taken from the thinking and mapping done for the curriculum trail. A Big Idea in the systems example is the interactivity and interdependence of animals, plants, and their environment.

Step 2: Identify Understanding Goals for a Project or Lesson. Understanding goals stem from Big Ideas. Therefore, to identify them, the teacher reviews the Big Idea or Ideas and focuses on what learners should know about them. In the example les-

FIGURE 8.3. Ant Nest Mural from Ron Buchanan's Kindergarten Classroom

son, the understanding goals could be grasping how animals (ants) live and work together in their environment. Ants are particularly good exemplars of animal systems because they live in obvious interactive communities and construct tangible artifacts of collaboration (ant hills with tunnels and chambers).

Step 3: Develop Generative Questions. Generative questions are created by putting the understanding goals into question form. How do animals (ants) live and work together? How do they respond to and shape their environment? What is an ecosystem? How can mapping our classroom (as artist-cartographers) help us learn about ants and ourselves? These questions should get learners wondering.

Step 4: Develop a Lesson or Project Idea. For this step the teacher should think about how best to explore the topic. She or he could revisit the through-line, particularly if it involves investigating processes, content, and how artists approach that content. Some art activity ideas can be derived from the creative strategies discussed in Chapter 7. Using art strategies is important for the systems example because the throughline is *Artists explore and interpret our interconnected world.* In the ant nest lessons, learners use the creative strategies of mapping and metaphor, since their classroom is cast as ant farm or nest. They also envision, explore, and reflect, three studio habits of mind (Hetland et al., 2013; Hogan et al., 2018). Reflection here enables learners to address the fourth generative question about how artists learn through mapping and metaphor.

Step 5: Develop the Lessons and Projects Further. The next step is to develop the lesson/project ideas further. The teacher should first design the core activities (the performances of understanding) in each lesson/project. In this example, Lesson 5, the activities involve creating a floor plan (map) of the classroom. Once the core activities are established, scaffolding activities are devised for each lesson/project that will engage learners and prepare them for the core of the lesson. Although they often occur at the beginning of a lesson or project, scaffolding activities can also be sprinkled throughout the work. These activities can include "book research," concept mapping of what children already know and what they want to learn about the subject, group discussions about the subject, and analyzing artworks or other resources that relate to the subject. In the systems curriculum here, scaffolding activities can also be one or more lessons that precede the mapping lesson, that is, Lessons 3 and 4, watching ants at work in the ant farm and making an art nest mural (see Figure 8.3).

More activity/scaffolding ideas can arise from the methods of various disciplines. What do professionals do when they begin their inquiries? For the ant farm mapping example, learners could mimic anthropologists. They could observe their classroom activities, the artifacts in the classroom, and the way the classroom is arranged. They could practice their storytelling skills by telling stories about what it would be like to be an ant or what they do in their classroom.

It is often difficult to tell the difference between scaffolding activities and the central activities in a project or lesson. That is because both are active learning experiences and build understanding while demonstrating understanding. Both are steps along the inquiry trail. The distinction lies in that the core activities in a lesson/project are the focal point of the project, whereas generative scaffolding activities prepare learners to enter into the core activities.

Scaffolding activities bring depth and breadth to a project, they give learners personal experiences with ideas and topics, they challenge learners to think about them, and they provide opportunities for learners to generate ideas they can employ in the core work. It should be noted that these activities are far more impactful if they are followed up with reflection.

Step 6: Devise Reflection Activities. After thinking through and designing the scaffolding and the core activities, the teacher devises the reflection activities. These activities can be answering reflection questions and documenting what occurred in the project or investigation. Reflection does not have to be a review of the project distinct from the art process or artworks, however. It can also be a creative extension of the project in which learners make an auxiliary artwork that entails reflecting on and explaining the concepts in the artwork and lessons. In the systems example, reflection could include navigating the classroom floor plan and acting as ants in the maze of paths and chambers (Lesson 6 in the example inquiry trail). Reflection could also be the storytelling activity described above. Examples of art-based reflection are illustrated in Chapter 9: the guidebook to the society learners create for Trail #3, and the packaging and care instructions for seeds and plants they prepare for Trail #4.

Closing Thoughts

I cannot overstate how important questioning is to all phases of a curriculum and the specific lessons or projects in it. Indeed, asking questions, tailoring them to the phases of a project (generative, guiding, and reflection questions) and also mixing them throughout the activities, makes the project and the entire curriculum workable and meaningful. It is also essential to challenge and enable students to develop their own questions, which they can ask themselves and their peers in critiques or discussions. Developing good questions can be a challenge. For that reason, ideas for generative, guiding, and reflection questions are included with the project trails illustrated in Chapter 9.

NEXT I provide five examples of creative inquiry project trails. These trails model how ideas can extend from one project to another and how this extension pushes a topic further to add meaning or to help learners see the topic in a more holistic way.

9

Inquiry Trails

Examples of Creative Inquiry-Based Art Integration

THIS CHAPTER describes five integrated art-inquiry project trails, each of which follows a theme across disciplinary boundaries and is developed according to the Teaching for Understanding (TfU) guidelines discussed in Chapter 8. After the project-trail descriptions, I offer remarks to conclude this book.

TRAIL #1: PATTERNS AND MATHEMATICS IN NATURAL FORMS

Overview

Learners will investigate basic forms in vegetables, flowers, leaves, and fruit (circles, spirals, branching, and webbing). They will observe the mathematics and symmetry in these forms and create their own cross-section of a vegetable or fruit. Then they will map the veins in their hands. They also will observe molds growing in petri dishes and create molds out of paper, cloth, crochet, and assorted collage materials (see Figure 9.1).

Understanding Goals. Understand natural growth patterns and forms, and how scientists and mathematicians observe and interpret them. Understand how artists are inspired by them.

Generative Questions. What patterns and forms do we see in living things? How are these patterns similar? What is it about growth that causes these regular patterns? How do mathematicians and scientists figure out the mathematical formulas? How does making artworks about things we study help us understand them?

Academic Concepts and Subjects Addressed. *Mathematics:* Regular patterns in nature. The mathematics underlying natural forms and patterns. ***Botany and zoology:*** Organic growth patterns in plants and animals. *Geology:* Basic forms in Earth formations. *History:* The story of how knowledge of mathematics and nature was preserved and developed in the Arab world, Persia, and India before coming to Europe in the dawn of the Renaissance.

Connected Contemporary Art. The work of Zemer Peled, Elin Thomas, and Maria Penil Cobo and Mehmet Berkman.

Creative Strategies. Distill, translate, employ unusual materials, map, translate.

Resource Materials. Vegetables; fruits; leaves; pictures of natural forms such as spiderwebs, trees, and rivers.

Guiding Questions. What patterns and shapes do you see? Do you find these forms and patterns in different vegetables, flowers, plants, and fruits? Why do you think this happens? How are the horizontal forms and patterns different from the vertical ones? Why do you think this happens? How are natural patterns and forms used in art and design?

FIGURE 9.1. Map of Trail #1: Patterns and Mathematics in Natural Forms

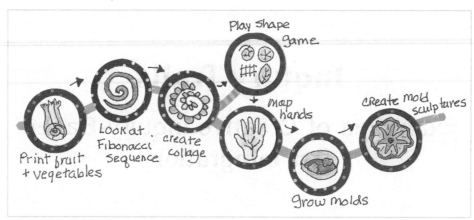

Performances of Understanding/ Studio Production

Lesson 1: Observe Basic Patterns in Plants.
The trail begins with the research question *What patterns and forms are inherent in living things?* To explore that question, learners print cross-sections of vegetables and fruits and take note of the spiral, circular, branching, and web patterns they discover (see Figure 9.2). Their attention is also directed toward radial and bilateral symmetry of vegetables and fruits, which are found in the same vegetable or fruit when they are sliced horizontally (radial) and vertically (bilateral) (see Figure 9.3).

Lesson 2: Explore Mathematical Relationships in Natural Patterns.
A close look at horizontal slices of fruits and vegetables sets the stage for exploring the mathematics behind spiral (gnomic growth) forms in many plants with related research into Fibonacci and the Fibonacci sequence (see Chapter 4).

The clearest displays of these forms and their regularity are found in flowers (such as roses and sunflowers), in succulents and pine cones, and in bunches of bok choy and celery.

Lesson 3: Create a Radial Form.
With different colors of paper, students invent their own succulents, flowers, or vegetables that spiral in a regular pattern according to the Fibonacci sequence.

Lesson 4: Play a Pattern-Recognition Game.
In this game, small groups of learners look at pictures of natural forms such as microbes, molds, plants, beehives, spiderwebs, whirlpools, hurricanes, rivers, trees, and lightning, which are shaped in spiral, branching, webbing, and radial formations. They then

FIGURE 9.3. Print Revealing the Fibonacci Spiral in Bok Choy and Fractal Branching in a Leaf

FIGURE 9.2. Plant Forms

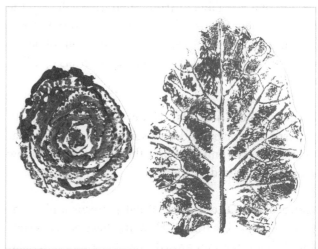

find pictures of man-made forms such as wheels, clocks, spiral staircases, fishing nets, knitted fabrics, family trees, street and highway maps, and scientific illustrations of life cycles, ecosystems, and computer networks. They then organize these images into a taxonomy of forms according to their shapes.

Lesson 5: Explore Branching and Webs. In this step, learners observe their palm lines and veins in one of their hands. They then outline their hand and map the branching patterns they see.

Lesson 6: Grow Natural Forms. Here, learners grow molds on agar in petri dishes and observe the spiral and branching patterns of the molds (refer to Figure 2.6, Maria Penil Cobo and Mehmet Berkman's *Brain Matter* [2018]).

Lesson 7: Create New Spiral and Branching Mold Forms. After observing the molds grow in their petri dishes, learners create their own clusters of molds. They can crochet or embroider these forms or make them out of clay, yarn, or paper (see Zemer Peled's *Everything Auspicious* [ND; Figure 9.4] and Elin Thomas's *Petri Dish Art* [ND; Figure 9.5]).

Reflection Questions

What did you learn about natural forms and patterns? What did you learn about math? How did exploring patterns, nature, and art through art making help you notice and understand them? What ideas are conveyed in your artwork? Where did those ideas come from? What forms and images did you use to convey your ideas? How did your ideas grow and change as you made your art? What did you learn about art or exploring nature through making art? With all that you have learned, what could you do next?

FIGURE 9.4. Zemer Peled, *Everything Auspicious* (ND)

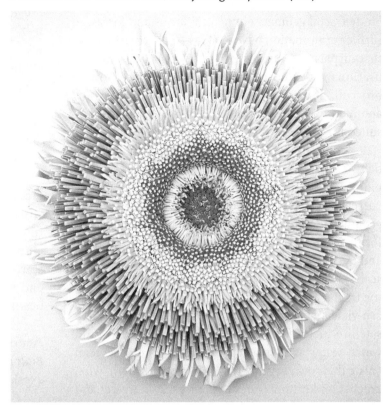

FIGURE 9.5. Elin Thomas, *Petri Dish Art* (ND)

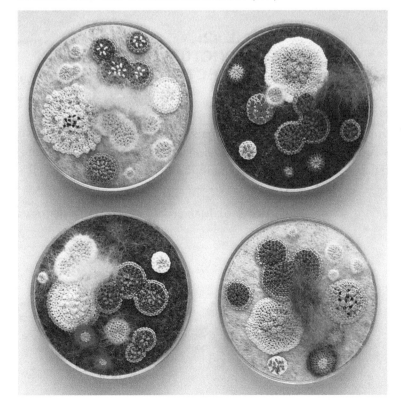

Possible Further Exploration

Study fractal geometry in natural forms and forces. A further examination of vegetables—particularly those that display complex branching patterns and configurations repeated at different scales (cauliflower, broccoli, and cabbages)—guides the inquiry toward another kind of geometry: fractals. This inquiry is best suited for 4th or 5th grades on up.

Fractal geometry describes mathematical patterns behind chaotic systems such as hurricanes, smoke plumes, lightning bolts, and turbulent liquids and air currents. It is also the geometry underlying complex geological forms such as rivers, coastlines, and rock formations, and self-similarity in cauliflower, brains, and trees (where the same form is repeated at different scales). To explore this geometry, learners can observe the fractal branching forms of corals and leaves. They can view maps of rivers and other landforms, observe satellite pictures of extreme weather patterns, and watch water as it splashes on the ground. They can create their own organic fractal forms with cloth, wire, crochet, or knitting (refer to Figure 4.2, Margaret and Christine Wertheim's Crochet Coral Reef project), or photograph and draw instances of fractal geometry they find in their environment, magazines, and books.

TRAIL #2: ANIMAL STRUCTURES AND ARCHITECTURE

Overview

Students will create four animals with four distinct structures: (1) invertebrate—sponges, worms, and jellyfish; (2) shelled animals—mollusks: bivalves or gas-tropods; (3) exoskeletons—insects, arachnids, and crustaceans; and (4) vertebrates—mammals, reptiles, fish, and amphibians. They will then apply their knowledge of these structures to architecture and create models of buildings with "soft" (inflatable), shell-like, exoskeletal, or skeletal structures (see Figure 9.6).

Understanding Goals. Understand four basic ways animals are structured. Understand how these forms are used in architecture and contemporary art.

Generative Questions. How are different animals structured? What is the connection between form and function? Why are animal species structured differently? How are artists, designers, and architects inspired by natural forms? How do architects use shells and skeletal structures to make buildings dynamic, beautiful, and strong?

Academic Concepts and Subjects Addressed. *Biology:* Structures of invertebrates, shelled animals, exoskeletal animals, and vertebrates.

Connected Contemporary Art and Architecture. Brian Jungen, sculptures *Cetology* (2002; refer to Figure 3.5) and *Carapace* (2009; refer to Figure 3.4); buildings by Santiago Calatrava, Frank Gehry and Javier Senosiain.

Creative Strategies. Translate, distill, mimic, juxtapose, extend, change scale.

Resource Materials. Shells and bones; photographs and scientific illustrations of human and animal skeletons, shells, invertebrates, mollusks, crus-

FIGURE 9.6. Map of Trail #2: Animal Structures and Architecture

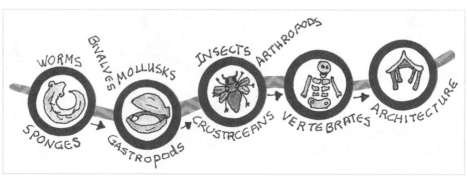

taceans, and insects; drawings and photographs of organic architecture.

Guiding Questions. What do you notice when you look at the four kinds of animals in this trail? How is each animal group different from the others? How do you make your own version of the animals and their structures? What can we invent and build using one of these structures? What structure works best for your architectural model? What materials will you use to build it?

Performances of Understanding/ Studio Production

Lesson 1: Research and Create Invertebrates. After researching invertebrates, such as jellyfish, microscopic animals, and worms, learners create soft, translucent animals out of plastic bags, balloons, clear package tape, translucent latex gloves, beads, plastic caps, ribbons, plastic tubing, and bubble wrap.

Lesson 2: Examine and Build Shells. Learners examine mollusks that live in shells. They create soft stuffed clams and oysters using felt, fiberfill, and collage materials such as plastic beads, sequins, and pompoms. They then build shells for their mollusks out of papier-mâché (newspaper strips infused with white glue or wallpaper paste). They do this by casting at least three layers of papier-mâché over balloons. After the shells are dry, cut open, and painted, learners place their soft stuffed animals inside them.

Lesson 3: Investigate and Create Exoskeletons (Arthropods). Learners investigate animals with exoskeletons: insects, arachnids, and crustaceans. They create their own exoskeletal animal by making a head, thorax, and abdomen in relief out of clay and then layering three layers of papier-mâché or paris-craft (plaster-infused cloth) over the clay. They create wings and six or eight legs, depending on the animal, out of pipe cleaners, wire, and tracing paper and attach them to the shell with hot glue or tape when the shell is dry and the clay has been removed. Once they paint the shell and attach the appendages, learners can cut and insert foam rubber into the exoskeleton to make the soft parts of the animal.

Lesson 4: Study and Construct Vertebrates. Learners study skeletons and make simplified skeletal armatures of soft wire or pipe cleaners. They can also construct heads in the same way they created shells for their mollusks. The next step is to wrap the skeletons with foam rubber and masking tape to create the muscles and flesh. These animals can be re-creations of living animals or the learner's fictional animal based on real skeletal structures. Another approach is to construct fantasy creature skeletons out of small found plastic objects using hot glue. A large version of this is Brian Jungen's *Cetology* (2002; refer to Figure 3.5).

Lesson 5: Observe Contemporary Architecture and Construct Models of New Buildings. Learners can look at the fantastical, organic skeletal buildings and bridges of architect Santiago Calatrava and the organic landscapes and structures inspired by seashells and other natural forms designed by Javier Senosiain. They can also observe architectural forms and structures such as tents, stadiums, high rises, huts, domes, and arches to find connections to the animal structures they investigated and created. In groups, learners then design and construct models of buildings, bridges, or other structures inspired by animal architecture.

Reflection Questions

What did you learn about animals and their structures? How did exploring these structures through making your own versions of them help you to understand them? What did you learn about structure and function? How did you improvise on these basic structures to create something new? How did your ideas grow and change as your work progressed and your artwork materialized? What did you learn about art, design, and architecture? Based on what you did in this series of projects, what could you do next?

Possible Further Exploration

Create costumes and body extensions based on exoskeletons out of stiff paper and masking tape or papier-mâché. For inspiration, students can study armor, particularly Japanese samurai armor and helmets.

FIGURE 9.7. Map of Trail #3: An Imaginary Island World

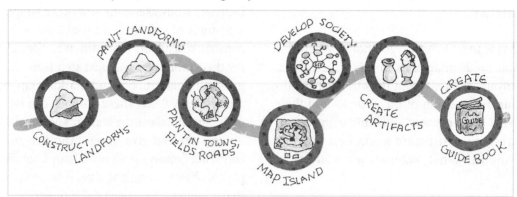

TRAIL #3:
AN IMAGINARY ISLAND WORLD

Overview

In groups of three or four, students will create an island civilization by constructing an island, mapping it, developing all the important components of a society, and making artifacts. They will then write and illustrate a guidebook to their island (see Figure 9.7).

Understanding Goals. Understand landforms and how they are shaped into various configurations by natural forces. Understand how the colors of a landscape are determined by the kinds of earth or vegetation on it, and how coloration is also governed by climate. Understand the effect of climate and terrain on a society. Understand the components and structures of a society, and how towns and surrounding areas are organized. Understand how art and artifacts represent daily life, societal values, and culture.

Generative Questions. What are the different landforms? How does its natural environment influence a civilization? Why are cities planned in different ways? What are the elements of a society and culture? How are these elements embodied in artifacts, art, and architecture? How do we represent a place, a society, a culture?

Academic Concepts and Subjects Addressed. *Geology:* Various landforms such as mountains, buttes, lakes, rivers, valleys, hills. *Environmental studies (ecology):* Climate, weather. *Geography and cartography.*

Social and cultural studies (anthropology): The physical and psychological characteristics of a place; the systems, institutions, values, and norms of a society and how they play out in the arts, fashion, architecture, and so forth. *Language arts:* The elements of language; storytelling and descriptive writing.

Connected Contemporary Art. Maya Lin, *Systematic Landscapes* (2006) and *2 × 4 Landscape* (2006); Luigi Serafini, *Codex Seraphinianus* (1981/2013); Bodys Isek Kingelez, *Kimbembele Ihunga* (1994); Mark Dion, *The Curiosity Shop* (2005) and *The Providence Cabinet* (2001).

Creative Strategies. Map, mimic, categorize, reformat, elaborate, extend, change scale, project, embody.

Resource Materials. Geological illustrations, weather maps, *Eyewitness* guidebooks, old maps. Harmon (2004, 2009); Miller (2016).

Guiding Questions. What places have you visited? What landforms have you seen in those places? How do you know if place is a desert or a jungle, a glacier, or a wetland? Have you ever flown over different landscapes? How did you know they were different? Where will you put your landforms, cities, farms, and roads? How will you represent your society in a map? What does your town or city have in it? How can a town or city be organized to make it livable? What are the important parts of a society? What are the important parts of a culture? What kinds of buildings does your society have? What values and spiritual traditions does your society have? What symbols represent the society? How do the objects produced and used in your society tell us about that world? How do buildings reflect the society? How do we explain and depict what people do, how they live, what they wear, what they care about, or how they are governed and organized?

Performances of Understanding/ Studio Production

Lesson 1: Build Land Forms. The trail begins with the research question *What are the different landforms?* Learners study landforms and then, in groups of 3 or 4, build islands out of ceramic clay. To save on clay, the islands can be made of clay slabs draped and shaped over wads of newspaper. From there, learners cover the islands with at least three layers of papier-mâché or pariscraft to create a shell.

Lesson 2: Create Climates and Environments. After the papier-mâché shell is dry and removed from the clay, students paint their landscapes. To determine the color scheme for their islands, learners look at how weather and climate determine vegetation and, therefore, coloration. They paint their islands according to the climate they have chosen. They paint in rivers, lakes, fields, and so forth. For this, I suggest that the groups be guided to choose different kinds of climates (tropical, desert, Arctic, arid, semitropical). This will provide variety in the islands and lead to more in-depth discussions of climate and its consequences.

Lesson 3: Paint in Details. In this step, learners decide what humans do on the islands and where the towns, roads, railroads, nations (if there are more than one), and so forth are located. They paint roads, trails, harbors, fields, and city sites on the landforms/islands.

Lesson 4: Map the Islands. Learners draw and paint maps of their islands that focus on details and provide information about the island. They use the conventions of cartography such as keys for information, symbols for different sites or places, and compasses.

Lesson 5: Develop Civilizations. Students determine the level of technology, kind of commerce and industry, form of government, and the values, art, literature, and spiritual traditions of their island civilizations. They can also design a set of symbols for flags and regalia for groups and officials.

Lesson 6: Create an Anthropology Museum. Learners create artifacts of the civilizations out of miscellaneous materials. They then label and display the artifacts. These can be costumes, household items, pictures of important political and cultural figures, samples of writing using the language of the island, pictures of people going about their daily lives, and symbolic objects.

Lesson 7: Prepare Travel Guides to or Ethnographies of the Islands. Students write and illustrate guides to their islands that include information about the government, people, commerce, arts, spiritual traditions, architecture, parks, food, clothing, animals, and important sites. Luigi Serafini's *Codex Seraphinianus* (Figure 9.8; also refer to Figures 6.4 and 6.5) is a model of a guide or anthropological study. The work is discussed in Chapter 6.

Reflection Questions

What did you learn about landforms and climate? How did making your own island help you understand how place, terrain, and climate determine how people live in a place? What did you learn about mapping as a way to think through, invent, and organize a place? What did you learn about societies and culture? How did you learn it? How did you improvise on ideas to create something new? How did your ideas grow and change as your work progressed and your island civilization materialized? How did making a guidebook or ethnography help you think through and invent a new place and culture? Where could you to go from here?

Possible Further Exploration

Develop an archaeological dig. Groups of three or more students build cities out of ceramic clay and

FIGURE 9.8. Luigi Serafini, Pages from the *Codex Seraphinianus* (1981/2013)

other materials in a large box or on a piece of plywood. They then map and paint the city streets and landmarks on the plywood or bottom of the box and then place their buildings on the plan. Next, students create miniature artifacts and other clues to their societies, such as scrolls with writing or pictures of daily life, which they sprinkle around the city. Each group should construct its city in secret. Once the cities are complete, students cover them with sand. As archaeologists, each group digs up another group's city. They label the artifacts and buildings they have found, write speculative explanations of the artifacts and the culture, and create archaeological displays.

FIGURE 9.9. Map of Trail #4: Medicinal Plants to Treat a Social Issue or Problem

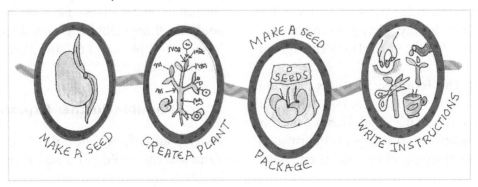

TRAIL #4:
MEDICINAL PLANTS TO TREAT
A SOCIAL ISSUE OR PROBLEM

Overview

Learners will create imaginary medicinal plants to treat social problems. They will make seeds, seed packets, and instructions for growing and using the plants (see Figure 9.9).

Understanding Goals. Understand the structure and function of seeds and plants. Understand medicinal plants and their powers. Understand how scientific illustration conveys information about a subject and how it can be used as a tool to invent something new and elaborate on it. Understand social issues and problems. Understand how plants provide metaphors for life, growth, and change that can be applied to social problems and issues. Understand how artists convey information and tell stories through visual formats and forms taken from scientific illustration and commercial packaging. Understand how imagination, invention, and creative thinking can generate deeper thinking about problems and solutions for them.

Generative Questions. What is a seed and why do plants have seeds? How do medicinal plants help us stay healthy or heal us when we are sick? How can we apply ideas and knowledge from one area (in this case, botany and medicine) to a problem in another area (social problems and issues)? How does this application help us to think creatively about problems and solutions? How do artists and scientists develop and convey information through annotated illustrations, maps, and diagrams?

Academic Concepts and Subjects Addressed. *Botany:* The structure and function of seeds and plants, medicinal plants, botanical illustration. *Social studies:* Social issues and problems and possible remedies for them. *Language arts:* Descriptive writing and storytelling.

Connected Contemporary Art. Nuala O'Donovan, ceramic seeds and plants; Tracey Bush, collage botanical illustrations.

Creative Strategies. Reformat, elaborate, project, extend, employ a metaphor.

Resource Materials. Botanical illustrations of medicinal plants, illustrated seed packets.

Guiding Questions. What do you notice when you look at a seed (its form, texture, structure, and color)? Why do you think a seed has these particular traits? What do you see when you dissect and observe the parts of a plant? What are the functions of the parts of a plant? What is a medicinal plant? Have you ever used one? What social issue or problem bothers you? What ideas do you have for solving this problem? If you had a medicinal plant that could solve the problem or treat its symptoms, what would it be like? What parts would it need? How would the plant work? How can you tell about the plant (its parts, attributes, and functions) through visual images and words? How would you grow it, care for it, and use it? How could you show this in instructions and packaging?

Performances of Understanding/ Studio Production

Lesson 1: Construct a Seed. The project begins with learners constructing seeds for their plants out of ceramic clay or papier-mâché. For this, they look at various seeds and seedpods.

Lesson 2: Invent Medicinal Plants. Learners concept map multiple social problems or issues for which they would like to find solutions. These issues can range from environmental issues like air pollution and species extinction, to problems humans have communicating or understanding each other, to making their school or community better. They then look at medicinal plants. Using these plants as models, learners invent their own plants to treat social issues or problems. Learners illustrate their plants using the visual language and formats of scientific illustration to designate the plant's parts, their structures and traits, and how they function. Here the process of drawing and mapping is a vehicle for invention.

Lesson 3: Make Seed Packets. Learners design and make packets for their seeds with illustrations of their plants and descriptions of what they do and how they work.

Lesson 4: Write Packet Instructions. Learners describe the care and use of their plants and attach the instructions to their seed packages.

Reflection Questions

What did you learn about plants and seeds? How did exploring plants and seeds through making models and scientific illustrations of them help you understand plants and seeds better? How did illustrating them this way help you work through ideas, invent a new plant, and tell about it? What ideas are conveyed on your seed packet and in your instructions? Where did you get your ideas? What images did you use to convey your ideas? How did your ideas grow and change as your artwork and invention materialized? What did you learn about the creative application of an idea to something seemingly unrelated? From what you learned and did in this project, what other artwork would you like to do? Where could this project go next?

Possible Further Exploration

Dissemination of wishes. Learners make hollow seed-pods out of tape, paper, pipe cleaners, and felt, making sure there is an opening in the pod. They attach a Velcro dot to the pod. They then write a wish on a strip of paper and place it in the pod. They stick the pod onto a friend, who reads the wish, puts the wish back into the pod (or adds a new wish), and passes the pod on to another friend.

TRAIL #5: ME AND MY WORLD

Overview

This extended trail explores the artist-learner's personal and cultural identity and how his or her identity is shaped by asking three basic questions. The throughline of the trail is "systems" and how each individual is a physical and psychological system nested within multiple social, cultural, and environmental systems.

The form of this trail reflects the content and the underlying trajectory of the curriculum. This is a trail that expands outward from a central point. Therefore, it is represented as a series of concentric circles (see Figure 9.10).

Understanding Goals. Learners will understand what systems are, how each person's body is a physical system, and how each individual lives within and is shaped by the social, cultural, and environmental systems in which they live.

Generative Questions. What am I? Who am I? What makes me who I am? (Each question will be addressed separately below.)

Academic Concepts and Subjects Addressed. *Natural sciences:* Natural systems in the body. *Social studies:* Cultural and social systems and groups that shape an individual. *Language arts:* Biography and fantasy.

Connected Contemporary Art. Fred Tomaselli, *Saint Utah with Flowers* (1996), *Before and After Saint Utah,* (2000), *Desert Bloom* (2000); Kerry James Marshall, *Untitled (Painter)* (2009), *Past Times* (1997), *School of Beauty, School of Culture* (2012); Robert Arneson, *Portrait of the Artist as a Clever Old Dog* (1981; refer to Figure 7.9), *Huddle* (1997); Mark Dion, *Threatrum Mundi Armarium* (2001).

Creative Strategies. Employ a metaphor, mimic, categorize, project, map, personify, extend, elaborate, employ metaphor.

Resource Materials. Anatomical illustrations, stethoscopes, magnifying glasses, timeline maps, pictures of historical and cultural figures.

Performances of Understanding/ Studio Production

> ## GENERATIVE QUESTION A: What Am I?

To answer this question, learners explore their bodies and the ways they reveal how everybody is a living system.

FIGURE 9.10. Map of Trail #5: Me and My World

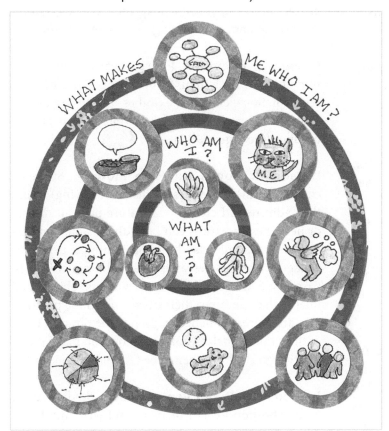

Guiding Questions for Exploring Generative Question A. What do I see? What do I hear? How does observing closely help me to understand what I am? How do all the parts of me fit and work together? How do I take what I observe about my body and create a story or new way of looking at it?

Lesson 1: Examine Hands. Students examine their hands with magnifying glasses and draw the veins or lines in their palms. They then visit a garden or vegetable market to observe and draw branching patterns in plants.

Lesson 2: Record Rhythms. Learners monitor their heartbeats and breathing with stethoscopes. They visualize these patterns by making a mark with paint on paper with each heartbeat or with each inhale and exhale.

Lesson 3: Consider Body Interiors. With an anatomical illustration as their guide, learners illustrate the interior of their bodies and write the fantasy journal of a microscopic explorer touring their bodies and visiting each organ.

Reflection Questions for Generative Question A. What did I learn about myself, my body, and how all the parts of me work together? How did I learn about this?

> **GENERATIVE QUESTION B: Who Am I?**

To explore this question, the inquiry turns toward the learner-artist's life.

Guiding Questions for Exploring Generative Question B. What objects do I own, use, and treasure? What is important about them? What stories could they tell? What do they reveal about me? What are the important events in my life and in what order did they happen? How do I show this in symbols? How do I show this on a timeline map? How did these experiences make me who I am? What memory stands out to me? What impossible (or possible), fanciful, or marvelous thing would I like to do?

Lesson 1: Attend to Personal Objects. Learners draw, concept map, and "interview" tools or other personal objects they use every day. They then write and illustrate biographies of their tools/objects with explanations of their use and significance. For a similar project, see Figures 7.25 and 7.26.

Lesson 2: Create an Exhibit. Learners make miniature clay replicas of their favorite objects from their past or present, and then make museum-style displays of them, complete with labels, descriptions, dates, curator's statements, and illustrated catalogs of their exhibits.

Lesson 3: Make Timeline Maps. Learners list important events in their lives and draw symbols of them on timelines. These timeline trails can take any form: circles, spirals, branching patterns, meanders, or webs. Here learner-artists can look at patterns in nature for inspiration.

Lesson 4: Make Collages of Memories and Fantasies. Learners create pairs of collages, with each pair including an illustration of a memory and another of a fantasy.

Lesson 5: Make Metaphorical Self-Portraits. Learners draw simple self-portraits (faces only). They then decide what animal, plant, machine, building, landform, or natural phenomenon would be an apt metaphor for them. They create a metaphorical self-portrait using the face drawing and embellishing it with the attributes of their metaphor. They can concept map this metaphor to explore its implications (refer to Figures 7.16 and 7.17).

Reflection Questions for Generative Question B. How do my personal objects reflect me and my life? How does mapping my life help me to think about what I have done, where I have been, what is happening now, and where I may be headed? How are my memories different from my fantasies? How does seeing myself as something else (that I am like) help me to understand myself?

➤ GENERATIVE QUESTION C: What Makes Me Who I Am?

Here the inquiry expands beyond the individual to culture, the human network in which the individual lives, and his or her physical and social environment.

Guiding Questions for Exploring Generative Question C. Who is in my family? Who are my friends? Who do I know from my school and neighborhood? How are all these people connected to me and to each other? What popular culture characters or stars, objects, or clothes are most popular with my friends and me? Who do I admire and why? What are the most important physical traits of this person? How do I represent her or him in symbols, a metaphor, or objects?

Lesson 1: Make a Concept Map of Relationships. Students concept map their friends, family, and acquaintances according to their relationships.

Lesson 2: Focus on Peers. Learners interview their peers about their favorite pop stars, movies, music, fictional characters, clothes, and TV programs; analyze the "data"; and make illustrated charts of their findings (see Figure 9.11).

Lesson 3: Focus on Role Models. Students choose a well-known person (historic or living) whom they admire and create a caricature portrait of him or her. These portraits can be 3-dimensional papier-mâché or ceramic clay busts or paintings, prints, or collages. Students research their role models' ideas, passions, and lives. They create symbolic objects and images that represent their lives. Since these portraits are caricatures, students exaggerate the physical traits of their role models. Another option is to make metaphorical portraits of them (see Question B, Step 5).

Lesson 4: Visit an Event or Place. Students go to a neighborhood event or place and write brief ethnographies about the experience and photograph and draw pictures of what they witness there. These visual and verbal ethnographies should include descriptions and drawings or photographs of the place, people, and activities learners observed.

Lesson 5: Engage in a Culminating Activity. Learners make a concept map of themselves with three concentric circles: the circle closest to the center for what I am (the body); the next circle out for who I am (close social circle, memories, and artifacts) and the outer circle for what makes me who I am. In Figure 9.12, this complex idea is distilled into "I care about."

Reflection Questions for Generative Question C. What did I learn about myself? How did I learn it? How did creating all the artworks in this trail build a "portrait" of me? How does making art about me, my social circle, and my life help me think about who I am, what is important to me, and where I fit into the world?

FIGURE 9.11. Rhea Dhar, *Who's Your Favorite Vampire?*

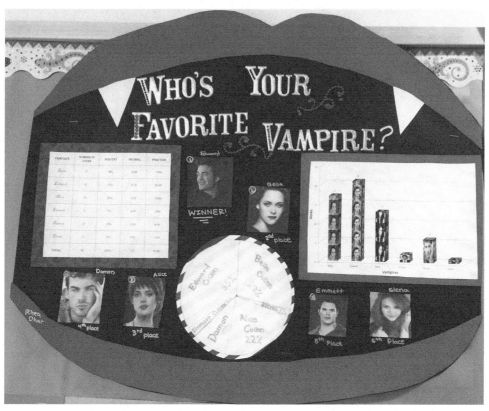

FIGURE 9.12. Miles Bourke, Concept Map: *I Care About*

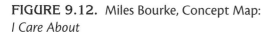

Possible Further Exploration

There are many ways to explore identity that can build on this inquiry trail. Students could personify an internal organ and write an illustrated story or comic book from its point of view. They could paint self-portraits of what they want to be in the future and write memoirs of their projected lives from the vantage point of their older selves. Students could create portraits of themselves with body extensions or prosthetics—such as wings, extra arms, multiple hands, wheels, stilts, or extra heads—that symbolize powers they would like to possess. An alternative to this is to make these wearable body extensions out of stiff paper, masking tape, and collage materials.

Conclusion

THIS BOOK concentrates on how integration through art-based inquiry fosters thinking, learning, and understanding. These are the cognitive rewards of the methodology. There are social and emotional rewards as well. Although the social and emotional benefits stem from art-based learning about how to think, learn, and create, they are not afterthoughts or side effects but are fundamental reasons why this approach has such promise. Indeed, they are the reasons why we do it.

The *Integrated Learning Goals* of the Integrated Learning Specialist Program (ILSP) in Alameda County, California, articulate the interconnectedness of the cognitive, social, and emotional aspects of integrated learning (Music et al., 2019). The goals are for each learner to

- Inquire creatively
- Think systemically
- Understand academic knowledge and disciplines
- Make personal meaning
- Think flexibly
- Be open, curious, and resilient
- Be metacognitive

- Develop care and the motivation to learn and act
- Think critically and independently
- Work collaboratively, collectively, and interdependently

I conclude with this list of goals because they not only connect the cognitive with the emotional and the social aspects of learning, but they also link understanding to empathy for others and a sense of agency and self-worth. I am convinced that through understanding come empathy and care for others; through play and freedom come motivation, knowledge, and curiosity; through thinking metacognitively come self-confidence, a sense of authorship and responsibility, and a reliance on oneself; through creative inquiry come flexibility, resourcefulness, and the ability to embrace change and the unknown; and through collaboration and sharing of ideas comes the ability to learn from others and to be with others. I believe all of these important cognitive, emotional, social, and behavioral traits and capacities are achievable. Moreover, they are key to more inclusive, humanistic, and joyful classrooms. Integration through creative arts-based inquiry is the best way I know to realize them. If you agree, join us and try it out. Happy Trails.

Credits

Figure 1.1. Map of a Creative-Inquiry Trail. By Julia Marshall.

Figure 1.2. Map of the Recursive Process of Creative Inquiry. By Julia Marshall.

Figure 1.3. Model Showing Learners' Initial Thinking About the Idea of Community. Creative Arts Charter School. Courtesy of Gina Griffiths and Ann Ledo-Lane.

Figure 1.4. Recording How Students Used the Studio Habits of Mind. Creative Arts Charter School. Courtesy of Gina Griffiths and Ann Ledo-Lane.

Figure 1.5. Imitating Buildings. Creative Arts Charter School. Courtesy of Gina Griffiths, Ann Ledo-Lane, and Ron Buchanan.

Figure 1.6. Exploring and Learning Through Mapping. Creative Arts Charter School. Courtesy of Gina Griffiths, Ann Ledo-Lane, and Ron Buchanan.

Figure 1.7. Zita Vitola-Giorni, Self-Portrait as a Neighborhood Helper. Creative Arts Charter School. Courtesy of the artist.

Figure 1.8. Vita Cuellar, Juniper Ximm, Adeline Foster, and Angelo Barillas, Illustrated Books About Neighborhood Helpers. Creative Arts Charter School. Courtesy of the artists.

Figure 1.9. Luma Ayish, "I Would Be the Fire House . . . I Am a Helper." Creative Arts Charter School. Courtesy of the artist.

Figure 1.10. Luma Ayish, Firehouse. Creative Arts Charter School. Courtesy of the artist.

Figure 1.11. The Streets That Connect Us. First-grade class, Creative Arts Charter School. Courtesy of the Gina Griffiths, Ron Buchanan, and Ann Ledo-Lane.

Figure 1.12. Map of the Cycle of Knowledge Construction. By Julia Marshall.

Figure 1.13. Raul's Maps of the Brain (**A**) Learning (Connecting) and (**B**) Not Learning (Not Connecting). Glen Park Elementary School, San Francisco. Courtesy of Linsey Weizenberg Larimore.

Figure 2.1. Timea Tihanyi, *Cosmology for a Skeptic* (2015). Courtesy of the artist. Photo by Timea Tihanyi.

Figure 2.2. Jane Hammond, *My Heavens* (2004). Courtesy of the artist.

Figure 2.3. Justin Lee, *Warrior* (ND). Courtesy of the artist.

Figure 2.4. Hine Mizushima, *Unnatural History Museum (Giant Daphnias)* (ND). Courtesy of the artist.

Figure 2.5. Hine Mizushima, *Unnatural History Museum (Giant Paramecium)* (ND). Courtesy of the artist.

Figure 2.6. Maria Penil Cobo in collaboration with Mehmet Berkman, *Brain Matter* (2018). Courtesy of the artists.

Figure 2.7. Amy Youngs, *Cute Parasites* (2008). Courtesy of the artist.

Figure 2.8. Scott Musgrove, Page from *Specious Beasts, An Introduction*. From *The Late Fauna of Early North America* (Musgrove, 2009). Courtesy of the artist.

Figure 3.1. Santiago Ramón y Cajal, *Purkinje Cell* (1899). Courtesy of the Cajal Institute, Cajal Legacy, Spanish National Research Council (CSIC), Madrid, Spain.

Figure 3.2. Matteo Farinella, Page from *Neurocomic* (Farinella & Roš, 2013, p. 16). Courtesy of the artist.

Figure 3.3. Bernie Lubell, *Up in the Air/Le Canard* (2015). Courtesy of Southern Exposure/Photograph by Matt Shapiro.

Figure 3.4. Brian Jungen, *Carapace* (2009). Courtesy of the artist and Catriona Jeffries Gallery.

Figure 3.5. Brian Jungen, *Cetology* (2002). Plastic chairs, 161.54 × 1260.40 × 168.66 cm. Collection of the Vancouver Art Gallery. Purchased with the financial support of the Canada Council for the Arts Acquisition Assistance Program and the Vancouver Art Gallery Acquisition Fund, VAG 2003.8 a-z. Courtesy of the artist and Catriona Jeffries Gallery. Photo by Trevor Mills, Vancouver Art Gallery.

Figure 3.6. Michael Arcega, *Auspicious Clouds | Heavy Fog* (2018). Ramona Arcega is sitting on the piece. Courtesy of the artist. Photo by Michael Arcega.

Figure 3.7. Shawn Lani, *Geyser* (2013). Courtesy of the Exploratorium, San Francisco, CA. Photo by Amy Snyder, © Exploratorium, www.exploratorium.edu

Figure 3.8. Fred Tomaselli, *Big Bird* (2004). Courtesy of the artist and James Cohan Gallery, New York.

Figure 3.9. Tony Cragg, *Spyrogyra* (1992). Sir Tony Cragg (England, b. 1949), *Spyrogyra* 1992, glass and steel, 220 × 210 cm. Art Gallery of New South Wales. Mervyn Horton Bequest Fund 1997 © Anthony Cragg. Photo: Diana Panuccio, AGNEW 292.1997.

Figure 3.10. Jason Freeny, *Cootie* (ND). Courtesy of the artist.

Figure 4.1. Timea Tihanyi, *Burst and Follow, Control and Release* (2018). *Viral Version Rule #5* (2018). 3D printed porcelain, mirrorized acrylic, 26 × 30 × 13". Photo Credit: Timea Tihanyi.

Figure 4.2. *Irish Satellite Reef* from the Crochet Coral Reef project by Margaret and Christine Wertheim and the Institute for Figuring.

Figure 4.3. Erik Demaine and Martin Demaine, *Destructor IV,* from the *Destructor* Series (2013–2015). Artwork and photograph by Erik Demaine and Martin Demaine. See http://erik demaine.org/curved/

Figure 4.4. Concept Map of Two. By Julia Marshall.

Figure 5.1. Njideka Akunyili Crosby, *"The Beautyful Ones" Series #4* (2015). Acrylic, color pencil, and transfers on paper. 61 × 42⅛" © Njideka Akunyili Crosby. Courtesy the artist, Victoria Miro Gallery, and David Zwirner.

Figure 5.2. Michael Rakowitz, from *The Invisible Enemy Should Not Exist* (2007–ongoing). Courtesy of the artist and Galerie Barbara Wien, Berlin. Photo by Nick Ash.

Figure 5.3. Wendy Red Star, *Peelatchiwaaxpáash / Medicine Crow (Raven),* from *The 1880 Crow Peace Delegation* Series (2014). Courtesy of the artist.

Figure 5.4. Britta Marakatt-Labba, *History* (2003–2007). Courtesy of the artist. Photo by Julia Marshall.

Figure 5.5. Paula Scher, *USA Extreme Weather* (2015). Courtesy of the artist and Pentagram Design.

Figure 5.6. Stephanie Syjuco, *Money Factory (An Economic Reality Game), Taiwan Biennial* (2015). Courtesy of the artist. Photo by Stephanie Syjuco.

Figure 6.1. Benny Andrews, *Harlem USA,* from the *Migrant* Series (2004). © 2018 Estate of Benny Andrews/Licensed by VAGA at Artists Rights Society (ARS), NY, Courtesy Michael Rosenfeld Gallery, LLC, New York, NY.

Figure 6.2. Mark Ryden, *The Apology* (2006). © Mark Ryden. Image Courtesy Kasmin Gallery.

Figure 6.3. Kerry James Marshall, *Souvenir II* (1997). © Kerry James Marshall, Courtesy of the artist and Jack Shainman Gallery, New York.

Figure 6.4. Manipulation of Rainbows: Pages from Luigi Serafini's *Codex Seraphinianus* (1981/2013). Courtesy of the artist.

Figure 6.5. Escaping Trees: Pages from Luigi Serafini's *Codex Seraphinianus* (1981/2013). Courtesy of the artist.

Figure 7.1. Map of the Concrete–Abstract Trail. By Julia Marshall.

Figure 7.2. Dawn Ng, *Walter: Somewhere Over a Concrete Rainbow* (2010). Courtesy of the artist.

Figure 7.3. Joyce Hsu, *Incomplete Metamorphosis* (ND). Courtesy of the artist. Photo by Julia Marshall.

Figure 7.4. Joan Brown, *The Bride* (1970). © The Estate of Joan Brown, courtesy of George Adams Gallery, New York.

Figure 7.5. Scott Musgrove, *The Late Fauna of Middle America* (2009). From *The Late Fauna of Early North America: The Art of Scott Musgrove* (Musgrove, 2009). Courtesy of the artist.

Figures 7.6. Bill Burns, from the *Safety Gear for Small Animals* Series (1994). Courtesy of the artist.

Figure 7.7. Ellen Jewett, *The White Stag* (2014). Courtesy of the artist.

Figure 7.8. Thomas Dambo, *Future Forest* (2018). Courtesy of the artist. Photo by www.thomasdambo.com

Figure 7.9. Robert Arneson, *Portrait of the Artist as a Clever Old Dog* (1981). Glazed ceramic, 32¾" × 18" × 30¼". Collection of Halley K. Harrisburg and Michael Rosenfeld, New York. Image courtesy of Michael Rosenfeld Gallery LLC, New York. © Estate of Robert Arneson/Licensed by VAGA at Artists Rights Society (ES), NY.

Figure 7.10. Maria Lai, *Bread Encyclopedia* (2008). © 2019 Artists Rights Society (ARS), New York/ADAGP, Paris.

Figure 7.11. Adam Dant, *Copenhagen* (2018). From *Living Maps: An Atlas of Cities Personified* (Dant, 2018). Courtesy of Chronicle Books LLC.

Figure 7.12. Simon Evans, *Survival* (2010). Courtesy of the artist and James Cohan Gallery, New York.

Figure 7.13. Tenmyouya Hisashi, *Adidas Superstar 2003 Version.* © TENMYOUYA Hisashi Courtesy of Mizuma Art Gallery.

Figure 7.14. David Hammons, *High Falutin'* (1990). © copyright *High Falutin'*. 1990 (some parts painted with oil), oil on wood, glass, rubber, velvet, plastic, and electric light bulbs, 13'2" × 48" × 30½" (396 × 122 × 77.5 cm). Robert and Meryl Meltzer Fund and purchase. Digital Image © the Museum of Modern Art/Licensed by SCALA/Art Resource, NY.

Figure 7.15. Thomas Dambo, *Bird House Mural* (2012). Courtesy of the artist. Photo by www.thomasdambo.com

Figure 7.16. Concept Map of Robert Arneson's *Portrait of the Artist as a Clever Old Dog.* By Julia Marshall.

Figure 7.17. Dinah Cooper, Concept Map of Robert Arneson's *Portrait of the Artist as a Clever Old Dog.* Creative Arts Charter School. Courtesy of the artist.

Figure 7.18. Summer Christensen, Concept Map of the Notion of Plant. Creative Arts Charter School.

Figure 7.19. *How Are All Our Issues Connected?* Collage Mural by Ms. Charpentier's 5th-Grade Class at Grattan Elementary School, San Francisco (2017). Courtesy Meredith Charpentier.

Figure 7.20. Lucy Shaw, Concept Map of a Plant from Her Research Workbook. Creative Arts Charter School. Courtesy of the artist.

Figure 7.21. Lucy Shaw, Scientific Drawings from Her Research Workbook. Creative Arts Charter School. Courtesy of the artist.

Figure 7.22. Lina Boyko, Map of the Life Cycle of a Plant from Her Research Workbook. Creative Arts Charter School. Courtesy of the artist.

Figure 7.23. Lucy Shaw, Reflections from Her Research Workbook. Creative Arts Charter School. Courtesy of the artist.

Figure 7.24. Lucy Shaw, Drawing of a Superpower Plant from Her Research Workbook. Creative Arts Charter School. Courtesy of the artist.

Figure 7.25. Sarah Knight-Weiss, Map of Her Key Chain. Francisco Middle School, San Francisco. Courtesy of the artist.

Figure 7.26. Kyle Chou, Concept Map of His Shoe. Francisco Middle School, San Francisco. Courtesy of the artist.

Figure 7.27. Sarah Knight-Weiss, Shoe Designs from Her Research Workbook. Francisco Middle School, San Francisco. Courtesy of the artist.

Figure 7.28. Kyle Chou, Map of Ideas and Concepts for Research. Courtesy of the artist.

Figure 7.29. Kyle Chou, Venn Diagram and Illustration of Ideas for Research. Courtesy of the artist.

Figure 8.1. Map of Teaching for Understanding Curriculum. By Julia Marshall.

Figure 8.2. Concept Map of a Project Trail Exploring Systems. By Julia Marshall.

Figure 8.3. Ant Nest Mural from Kindergarten Classroom. Creative Arts Charter School. Courtesy of Ron Buchanan.

Figure 9.1. Map of Trail #1: Patterns and Mathematics in Natural Forms. By Julia Marshall.

Figure 9.2. Plant Forms. Creative Arts Charter School.

Figure 9.3. Print Revealing the Fibonacci Spiral in Bok Choy and Fractal Branching in a Leaf.

Figure 9.4. Zemer Peled, *Everything Auspicious* (2015). Courtesy of the artist.

Figure 9.5. Elin Thomas, *Petri Dish Art* (ND). Courtesy of the artist.

Figure 9.6. Map of Trail #2: Animal Structures and Architecture. By Julia Marshall.

Figure 9.7. Map of Trail #3: An Imaginary Island World. By Julia Marshall.

Figure 9.8. Luigi Serafini, Pages from the *Codex Seraphinianus* (1981/2013). Courtesy of the artist.

Figure 9.9. Map of Trail #4: Medicinal Plants to Treat a Social Issue or Problem. By Julia Marshall.

Figure 9.10. Map of Trail #5: Me and My World. By Julia Marshall.

Figure 9.11. Rhea Dhar, *Who Is Your Favorite Vampire?* Cranbrook Kingswood Middle School for Girls, Bloomfield Hills, Michigan. Courtesy of the artist and Jane Shettel Williams, teacher.

Figure 9.12. Miles Bourke, Concept Map: *I Care About.* Creative Arts Charter School. Courtesy of the artist.

References

Aicken, F. (1991). *The nature of science*. Portsmouth, NH: Heinemann.

Ayers, R. (2014). Creative writing: The long and winding road. In J. Marshall & D. M. Donahue, *Art-centered learning across the curriculum: Integrating contemporary art in the secondary school classroom* (pp. 119–139). New York, NY: Teachers College Press.

Beane, J. (2011). Curriculum integration and the disciplines of knowledge. In J. Seften-Green, P. Thompson, K. Jones, & L. Bressler (Eds.), *The Routledge international handbook of creative learning* (pp. 193–199). London, UK: Routledge.

Ben-Ari, M. (2005). *Just a theory: Exploring the nature of science.* Amherst, NY: Prometheus.

Beveridge, W. I. B. (2004). *The art of scientific investigation.* New York, NY: Norton. (Original work published 1950)

Black, M. (1981). Metaphor. In M. Johnson (Ed.), *Philosophical perspectives on metaphor* (pp. 63–81). Minneapolis, MN: University of Minnesota.

Blythe, T., & Perkins, D. (1998). The teaching for understanding framework. In T. Blythe et al., *The teaching for understanding guide* (pp. 17–24). San Francisco, CA: Jossey-Bass.

Bohm, D. (1998). *On creativity.* London, UK: Routledge.

Boix-Mansilla, V., & Gardner, H. (1998). What are the qualities of understanding? In M. S. Wiske (Ed.), *Teaching for understanding: Linking research with practice* (pp. 161–183). San Francisco, CA: Jossey-Bass.

Bowers, M. A. (2004). *Magical realism.* New York, NY: Routledge.

Brown, T. (2003). *Making truth: Metaphor in science.* Urbana-Champaign, IL: University of Illinois.

Clark, E. T. (1997). *Designing and implementing an integrated curriculum: A student-centered approach.* Brandon, VT: Holistic Education Press.

Clark, R. P. (2016). *Writing tools: 55 essential strategies for every writer.* New York, NY: Little Brown.

Common Core State Standards Initiative. (2014). *Preparing America's students for success.* Available at www.corestandards.org

Cossey, R., & Donahue, D. M. (2014). Mathematics: Logic and imagination. In J. Marshall & D. M. Donahue, *Art-centered learning across the curriculum: Integrating contemporary art in the secondary school classroom* (pp. 140–160). New York, NY: Teachers College Press.

Csikszentmihalyi, M. (1996). *Creativity: Flow and the psychology of discovery and invention.* New York, NY: Harper Perennial.

Dant, A. (2018). *Living maps: An atlas of cities personified.* San Francisco, CA: Chronicle Books.

DeFelipe, J. (2010). *Cajal's butterflies of the soul: Science and art.* New York, NY: Oxford University Press.

Derry, G. (1999). *What science is and how it works.* Princeton, NJ: Princeton University.

Devlin, K. (1994). *Mathematics: The science of patterns.* New York, NY: Scientific American.

Devlin, K. (2000). *The math gene: How mathematical thinking evolved and why numbers are like gossip.* New York, NY: Basic Books.

Dewey, J. (1902). *The child and the curriculum.* Chicago, IL: University of Chicago.

Doll, W. E., Jr., Fleener, M. J., Trueit, D., & St. Julien, J. (Eds.). (2005). *Chaos, complexity, curriculum and culture: A conversation.* New York, NY: Lang.

Donahue, D., & Drouin, S. (2014). History: Making meaning of the past. In J. Marshall & D. M. Donahue, *Art-centered learning across the curriculum: Integrating contemporary art in the secondary school classroom* (pp. 82–104). New York, NY: Teachers College Press.

Ede, S. (2005). *Art and science.* London, UK: Taurus.

Efland, A. (2002). *Art and cognition: Integrating the visual arts into the curriculum.* New York, NY: Teachers College Press.

Farinella, M., & Roš, H. (2013). *Neurocomic.* London, UK: Nobrow.

Fink, L. D. (2013). *Creating significant learning experiences: An integrated approach to designing college courses.* San Francisco, CA: Jossey-Bass.

Finke, R., Ward, T., & Smith, S. (1996). *Creative cognition: Theory, research and application.* Cambridge, MA: MIT.

Fleener, M. J. (2005). Introduction. Chaos, complexity, curriculum, and culture: Setting up the conversation. In W. E. Doll, Jr., M. J. Fleener, D. Trueit, & J. St. Julien (Eds.), *Chaos, complexity, curriculum and culture: A conversation* (pp. 1–17). New York, NY: Lang.

Fosnot, C. T., & Perry, R. S. (2005). Constructivism: A psychological theory of learning. In C. T. Fosnot (Ed.), *Constructivism: Theory, perspectives, and practice* (2nd ed., pp. 8–38). New York, NY: Teachers College Press.

García Márquez, G. (1970). *One hundred years of solitude.* New York, NY: HarperCollins.

Gauch, H. (2012). *Scientific method in brief.* Cambridge, UK: Cambridge University.

Geertz, C. (1973). *The interpretation of culture.* New York, NY: Basic Books.

Gimbel, S. (Ed.). (2011). *Exploring the scientific method: Cases and questions.* Chicago, IL: University of Chicago.

Gnanakan, K. (2011). *Integrated learning.* New Delhi, India: Oxford University Press.

Gutkin, L. (2012). *You can't make this stuff up: The complete guide to writing creative nonfiction.* Philadelphia, PA: Da Capo Books.

Harmon, K. (2004). *You are here: Personal geographies and other maps of the imagination.* New York, NY: Princeton Architectural Press.

Harmon, K. (2009). *Map as art: Contemporary artists explore cartography.* New York, NY: Princeton Architectural Press.

Hart, J. (2011). *Storycraft: The complete guide to writing narrative nonfiction.* Chicago, IL: University of Chicago Press.

Hayakawa, S. I. (1939). *Language in thought and action.* San Diego, CA: Harcourt.

Hetland, L., Winner, E., Veneema, S., & Sheridan, K. M. (2013). *Studio thinking 2: The real benefits of visual arts education* (2nd ed.). New York, NY: Teachers College Press.

Hogan, J., Hetland, L., Jacquith, D. B., & Winner, E. (2018). *Studio thinking from the start: The K–8 art educator's handbook.* New York, NY: Teachers College Press.

Horvath, L., & Marshall, J. (2014). The natural sciences: Understanding the natural world. In J. Marshall & D. M. Donahue, *Art-centered learning across the curriculum: Integrating contemporary art in the secondary school classroom* (pp. 35–57). New York, NY: Teachers College Press.

Hunter-Koniger, T. (2018). Project-based learning: Using artistic pedagogies for educational leadership. *Art Education Journal, 71,* 46–51.

Kac, E. (Ed.). (2007). *Signs of life: BioArt and beyond.* Cambridge, MA: MIT.

Keller, R. (2015). *Excavating history: Artists take on historic sites.* Park Ridge IL: StepSister Press.

Kendall, D. (2012). *Sociology in our times.* Belmont, CA: Wadsworth.

Kirschner, P. A., Sweller, J., & Clark, R. E. (2006). Why minimal guidance during instruction does not work: An analysis of the failure of constructivist, discovery, problem-based, experiential and inquiry-based teaching. *Educational Psychologist, 41*(2), 75–86.

Kirst, W., & Dickmeyer, U. (1992). *Kreativitatstraining.* Reinbek bei Hamburg, Germany: Rowholt. (Original work published 1973)

Knox, P., & Martson, S. A. (2012). *Human geography: Places and regions in global context.* New York, NY: Pearson.

Kolencik, P., & Hillwig, S. (2011). *Encouraging metacognition.* New York, NY: Lang.

Krechevsky, M., Mardell, B., Rivard, M., & Wilson, D. (2013). *Visible learners: Promoting Reggio-inspired approaches in all schools.* San Francisco, CA: Jossey-Bass.

Kuhns, T. (1962). *The structure of scientific revolutions.* Chicago, IL: University of Chicago Press.

Lacy, S. (Ed.). (1995). *Mapping the terrain: New genre public art.* Seattle, WA: Bay Press.

Lacy, S. (ND). *Code 33: Emergency clear the air!* Available at suzannelacy.com/the-oakland-projects

Lakoff, G., & Johnson, M. (1980). *Metaphors we live by.* Chicago, IL: University of Chicago.

Latour, B. (1987). *Science in action.* Cambridge, MA: Harvard University Press.

Leal, L. (1995). Magical realism in Spanish American literature (1967). In L. P. Zamora & W. B. Faris (Eds.), *Magical realism: Theory, history, community* (pp. 119–124). Durham, NC: Duke University.

Lima, M. (2014). *The book of trees: Visualizing branches of knowledge.* New York, NY: Princeton Architectural Press.

Lima, M. (2017). *The book of circles: Visualizing spheres of knowledge.* New York, NY: Princeton Architectural Press.

Mandelbrot, B. B. (1983). *The fractal geometry of nature.* New York, NY: Henry Holt.

Marshall, J. (2014). The social sciences: Knowing ourselves and others. In J. Marshall & D. M. Donahue, *Art-centered learning across the curriculum: Integrating contemporary art in the secondary school classroom* (pp. 58–81). New York, NY: Teachers College Press.

Marshall, J., & D'Adamo, K. (2018). Art studio as thinking lab: Fostering metacognition in art classrooms. *Art Education, 71*(6), 9–16.

Marshall, J., & Donahue, D. M. (2014). *Art-centered learning across the curriculum: Integrating contemporary art in the secondary school classroom.* New York, NY: Teachers College Press.

Miller, L. (Ed.). (2016). *Literary wonderlands: A journey through the greatest fictional worlds ever created.* New York, NY: Black Dog and Leventhal.

Monaghan, J., & Just, P. (2000). *Social and cultural anthropology: A short introduction.* Oxford, UK: Oxford University.

Murphy, R. F. (1989). *Cultural and social anthropology: An overview.* Englewood Cliffs, NJ: Prentice Hall.

Musgrove, S. (2009). *The late fauna of early North America: The art of Scott Musgrove.* San Francisco, CA: Last Gasp.

Music, L., Noval, T., Marshall, J., Pine, G., Johnson, N., & Lee, M. (2019). *Integrated learning specialist handbook.* Hayward, CA: Department of Integrated Learning, Alameda County Office of Education.

Necka, E. (1986). On the nature of creative talent. In A. J. Cropley, K. K. Urban, H. Wagner, & W. H. Wieczerkowski (Eds.), *Giftedness: A continuing worldwide challenge* (pp. 131–140). New York, NY: Trillium.

Newton, R. (2012). *Why science? To know, to understand and to rely on results.* Singapore: World Scientific.

Next Generation Science Standards (NGSS). (2013). Available at nextgenscience.org

Orotony, A. (1993). Metaphor, language and thought. In A. Orotony (Ed.), *Metaphor and thought* (pp. 1–16). Cambridge, UK: Cambridge University.

Perkins, D. (1988). Art as understanding. In H. Gardner & D. Perkins (Eds.), *Art, mind and education: Research from Project Zero* (pp. 111–131). Chicago, IL: University of Illinois.

Piaget, J. (1955). *The child's construction of reality.* New York, NY: Routledge.

Pollman, M. J. (2017). *The young artist as scientist: What can Leonardo teach us?* New York, NY: Teachers College Press.

Prown, J. (2001). *Art as evidence: Writings on art and material culture*. New Haven, CT: Yale University Press.

Ricoeur, P. (1991). The function of fiction in shaping reality. In M. Valdez (Ed.), *A Ricoeur reader: Reflection and imagination* (pp. 117–136). Toronto, Canada: University of Toronto Press.

Ritchhart, R. (2015). *Creating cultures of thinking: The eight forces we must master to transform our schools*. San Francisco, CA: Jossey-Bass.

Ritchhart, R., Church, M., & Morrison, K. (2011). *Making thinking visible: How to promote engagement, understanding and independence for all learners*. San Francisco, CA: Jossey-Bass.

Samuel, N. (2014). A curatorial sketch. In G. Wittkopp & N. Samuel (Eds.), *My brain is in my inkstand: Drawing as thinking and process*. Bloomfield Hills, MI: Cranbrook.

Schneider, A., & Wright, C. (2010). *Between art and anthropology. Contemporary ethnographic practice*. Oxford, UK: Berg.

Serafini, L. (2013). *Codex Seraphinianus*. New York, NY: Rizzoli. (Original work published 1981)

Silver, N. (2013). Reflective pedagogies and the metacognitive turn in college teaching. In M. Kaplan, N. Silver, D. Lavaque-Manty & D. Meizlish (Eds.), *Using reflection and metacognition to improve student learning: Across the disciplines, across the academy* (pp. 1–17). Sterling, VA: Stylus.

Spronken-Smith, R., & Walker, R. (2010). Can inquiry-based learning strengthen the links between teaching and disciplinary research? *Studies in Higher Education, 35*(6), 723–740.

Strauss, M. J. (2013). Learning by drawing, thinking, and revising. In *The mind at hand: What drawing reveals. Stories of exploration, discovery and design* (pp. 23–38). Irvine, CA: Brown-Walker.

Sullivan, G. (2010). *Art practice as research: Inquiry in the visual arts*. Los Angeles, CA: Sage.

Trueit, D. (2005). Watercourses: From poetic to poietic. In W. E. Doll, Jr., M. J. Fleener, D. Trueit, & J. St. Julien (Eds.), *Chaos, complexity, curriculum and culture: A conversation* (pp. 77–99). New York, NY: Lang.

Turchi, P. (2004). *Maps of the imagination: The writer as cartographer*. San Antonio, TX: Trinity University Press.

Vygotsky, L. S. (2012). *Thought and language*. Cambridge, MA: MIT Press.

Wallas, G. (2014). *The art of thought*. Kent, UK: Solis.

Wertheim, M. (2015). Corals and mathematics. In M. Wertheim & C. Wertheim, *Crochet coral reef: A project by the Institute for Figuring* (pp. 42–47). Los Angeles, CA: Institute for Figuring.

Wiske, M. S. (1998). What is teaching for understanding? In M. S. Wiske (Ed.), *Teaching for understanding: Linking research with practice* (pp. 61–86). San Francisco, CA: Jossey-Bass.

Wormeli, R. (2009). *Metaphors and analogies: Power tools for teaching any subject*. Portland, ME: Stenhouse.

Index

The notation *f* following a page number refers to a figure on that page.

Biographical Notes

Author

JULIA MARSHALL is professor emeritus of Art Education at San Francisco State University in San Francisco, California, where she taught graduate and undergraduate courses. Before her tenure there, Julia was a teaching artist in Bay Area elementary and middle schools. Her publications include numerous chapters in art education anthologies and a variety of articles in *Studies in Art Education* and the *Art Education Journal*. She is coauthor with David M. Donahue of *Art-Centered Learning Across the Curriculum: Integrating Contemporary Art in the Secondary School Classroom* published by Teachers College Press.

Educators Who Guided Students in Work Featured Prominently in This Volume

ANN LEDO-LANE is an artist and arts-centered educator who is passionate about and committed to innovative, arts-integrated, project-based learning practices to nurture creative and equitable classrooms. Currently the director of Arts Programming at the Creative Arts Charter School in San Francisco, Ann holds a Master's of Education from Teachers College, Columbia University, and was a member of the 2017 cohort in the National Arts Educator Association's School for Art Leaders program. Since 2017, Ann has taught as an adjunct faculty member in the Education Department at San Francisco State University. Ann loves chairs, making books, and exploring nature and art with her family in San Francisco.

ELIZABETH McAVOY is a middle school visual arts teacher in San Francisco, California. She holds a Master's of Education from California State University San Marcos and a Bachelor's Degree in Journalism from San Francisco State University. Her most recent publication is a trifold guide titled *Mindfulness for Teachers and Students*. Liz loves teaching art-based research because her students have the space and time to develop their curiosity, perseverance, and creativity while delving deeply into a topic of their choosing.